Nonprofit Strategic Planning

Nonprofit Strategic Planning

Leveraging Sarbanes-Oxley
Best Practices

Peggy M. Jackson, DPA, CPCU

BICENTENNIAL
1807
WILEY
2007
BICENTENNIAL

John Wiley & Sons, Inc.

Library of Congress Cataloging-in-Publication Data:

ISBN: 978-0470-12076-7

Printed in the United States of America

10 9 8 7 6 5 4 3 2 1

This book is dedicated with gratitude to
Delia Fleishhacker Ehrlich
one of San Francisco's treasures.

Contents

Acknowledgments

I would like to thank my editor, Susan McDermott, and the wonderful staff at John Wiley & Sons for their help and support in the writing of this book.

I would also like to acknowledge the support and encouragement that I received from friends, family, and colleagues. Paul, Rick, Jan, and Gemma keep things in humorous perspective. You have been steadfast in cheering me on and a constant source of inspiration.

PMJ

About the Author

Dr. Peg Jackson is an author, consultant, and nationally recognized lecturer in risk management, business continuity planning, and Sarbanes-Oxley compliance. She earned a doctorate in public administration (DPA) from Golden Gate University in San Francisco and holds the professional designation of Chartered Property and Casualty Underwriter (CPCU). She designed the Jackson Risk Management Model© as part of an award-winning doctoral dissertation on risk management techniques. She has written *Sarbanes-Oxley for Nonprofits* and *Sarbanes-Oxley for Nonprofit Management*, both books co-authored with Toni E. Fogarty, PhD. She has also written *Nonprofit Risk Management and Contingency Planning: Done in a Day Strategies*, *Sarbanes-Oxley for Nonprofit Boards*, and *Sarbanes-Oxley for Small Businesses: Leveraging Compliance for Maximum Advantage*. She is a principal with Adjunct LLC in San Francisco, California.

Preface

The ancient Chinese proverb of "A journey of a thousand miles begins with a single step" could be applied to the strategic planning process. Would you even consider making a thousand-mile venture to a place you had never been without the aid of a good map? Or an airline ticket? Or a travel agent? Or a guide? That's what many nonprofits do when they attempt to engage in strategic planning without having the foggiest idea of what it is, why they are doing it, or where it will take them.

Nonprofits do have a way to prepare to engage in meaningful strategic planning. Sarbanes-Oxley (SOX) requirements and best practices facilitate the improvement of the nonprofit's operational systems, procedures, and methods for doing business. Further, engaging in SOX best practices activities will not only help your nonprofit to clean out the cobwebs, but it will help you to learn about how the nonprofit deals with solving problems and establishing important control mechanisms.

Strategic planning is an exciting endeavor that can become even more meaningful when your nonprofit is SOX compliant and ready to meet the future.

PMJ

CHAPTER 1

Why Nonprofits Waste Time, Money, and Energy in Strategic Planning

INTRODUCTION

Madeline was the new committee chair for the Prescott Hill Women's Society (PHWS) magazine. As she sat in her first meeting with the Society president, Honoria Newdough, and communications chair, Samantha Skreemer, Madeline was grilled on her knowledge of all things PHWS. The Society president glared at her icily and demanded to know how Madeline intended to use this year's magazine to report on the PHWS strategic plan. "What strategic plan?" Madeline asked.

"*You don't know??*" thundered Honoria.

"Sorry, but I really don't, and I'm not sure that anyone in PHWS does either."

Strategic planning consumes enormous amounts of resources in the nonprofit world annually. This translates into time, money, labor, energy, paper, electricity, use of meeting rooms, preparation of food, and other resources associated with the process. What's the return on this investment? Does anyone even think of the process as an investment and *expect a return?* Probably not.

How many times have you heard people in your nonprofit or in other nonprofits refer to the specific contents of their strategic plan—particularly when they are about to make a decision? Probably never. It's no surprise that nonprofit boards and leaders rarely mention the focus of the strategic plan or its vision for the nonprofit. It is also very unlikely that they understand how they are going to organize the nonprofit's resources to achieve goals of any kind.

What are some of the reasons why nonprofits engage in a process that often appears to produce few results while consuming significant time, staff, and monetary resources? Considering the relative scarcity of money within most nonprofit organizations, it is counterintuitive to see these organizations routinely squandering money on a process that they don't understand and for which they cannot identify any tangible—or even intangible—benefits. As incredible as this may seem, many nonprofits appear willing, if not eager, to toss good money after bad for the sake of "strategic planning."

WHY DO NONPROFITS WASTE RESOURCES TRYING TO WRITE STRATEGIC PLANS?

If nonprofits are willing to expend significant sums to create strategic plans that they intend to ignore, then why bother in the first place? Here are 30 reasons why nonprofits squander time, resources, and intellectual capital when they attempt to engage in strategic planning.

1. *The trade literature suggests that every nonprofit should engage in strategic planning.* There are books, magazine articles, web sites, lectures, conferences, and workshops all dedicated to helping nonprofits design strategic plans. The clear message in nonprofit trade magazines is that nonprofits all need to engage in routine strategic planning.

2. *The board expects the nonprofit to do strategic planning, and all of the other nonprofits seem to be drafting strategic plans.* The expectation that strategic planning is an essential component of nonprofit management is correct, presuming that the board and other decision makers understand why it should be done and what to do to make the plan work.

3. *Foundation requests for proposals (RFPs) might request a copy of the nonprofit's latest strategic plan.* Some organizations actually create strategic plans for the purpose of satisfying the requirements of a funder.

4. *Major donors may request a copy of the nonprofit's latest strategic plan.* This is a variation on Excuse 3, but in the case of the high-wealth donor, the nonprofit probably skews the findings of the strategic plan to suit the pitch that they want to make to the donor.

5. *It's a good way to secure a weekend retreat at a nice resort.* This reason may sound facetious, but the reality is that the quality of the plan is not ever contingent on the quality of the surroundings in which it was created.

6. *The nonprofit did not do its homework before the planning process began.* The nonprofit has no idea who its competitors are and how these competitors are faring compared to the nonprofit. Nonprofits do indeed have competitors for funding, board members, management, and other important organizational assets. Effective strategic planning includes environmental scanning.

7. *The nonprofit does not understand current trends in philanthropy.* Foundations and high-wealth donors will support those nonprofits that have gained their trust by solid management practices. The executive director of a historic nonprofit took one of the city's society doyennes to lunch to make a seven-figure pitch for the restoration of part of the nonprofit's building based on its recently drafted strategic plan. The socialite also happened to be an astute businesswoman. She told the executive director that she was not impressed with the way the nonprofit handled its finances. Period. The newly drafted strategic plan could not make up for years of what she saw as financial incompetence. The pitch for seven figures rendered $50,000.

8. *The nonprofit does not understand why certain nonprofits were funded by foundations, public grants, major donors.* Trends in philanthropy are signaled by the types of nonprofits and programs that are funded through traditional philanthropic channels.

9. *The nonprofit has no idea how it is perceived by its donors at all levels, nor does it have any idea how it as an institution is perceived by the public at large.* Nonprofits waste money and resources on strategic planning if they are not in touch with their donor base, community, and potential funders.

10. *The nonprofit does not have a plan to address contingencies.* What would happen to the nonprofit if a key executive left the organization, or a grant was not renewed, or a major donor stopped contributing?

Nonprofit strategic planning rarely identifies strategies for dealing with these very real contingencies.

11. *No one in the nonprofit's board or management really understands what these plans are about or how to execute the plan once it's written.* It's easier to hire a consultant from the local management clearinghouse to facilitate a few sessions, write something up, and be done with it. No one learns anything because, of course, no one wants to admit that they don't understand the utility of a strategic plan or how to execute one. This is one of the primary reasons why strategic planning becomes an exercise in futility.

12. *The plan does not clearly articulate goals, expected changes in productivity or behavior, expected changes in programmatic emphasis, or the types of resources necessary to bring about lasting change.* The nonprofit has not looked beyond its plan to see what it would take to actually achieve its strategic goals.

13. *The nonprofit's board, management, and employees do not understand how the organizational culture will need to change in order to accomplish the strategic plan's goals.* Strategic planning means that the nonprofit is ready to operate in a business like manner. Many nonprofits seem to be particularly skillful at coming up with elaborate fantasies about why they can't possibly run the organization like a business.

14. *The nonprofit does not understand how it will use a strategic plan.* The nonprofit believes it will always operate on a shoestring. This reason suggests that planning is directly correlated to financial status. The message is that there's no point to planning because the nonprofit will never have the resources to take the plan to fruition.

15. *We serve poor people, so that means we can't run the organization like a business.* This variation on Excuse 14 suggests that the quality of planning is directly related to the clients' socioeconomic status.

16. *We're grassroots, so if we run the organization like a business, we're selling out to the Establishment.* This excuse suggests that strategic planning is subversive because the nonprofit would be engaging in what they dismiss as private-sector activities.

17. *We're a volunteer organization—we don't have the time or the people to run this like a business.* Strategic planning will not work in an organization that is resistant to professional business practices.

18. *The strategic plan was written by consultants who did not take the time to do the necessary research to fully understand the nonprofit, its challenges, and its unique attributes.* The strategic plan that they facilitated looks just like any other plan they facilitated in the past and is meaningless to their current nonprofit client. The client wanted a strategic plan and was happy to outsource it. If no one knows what to do next, then nothing will get done! A shortcut that is resource consuming and short on results is hiring consultants who bring their one-size-fits-all strategic planning methods. The nonprofit is handed a strategic plan that someone else wrote. No one in the nonprofit has any investment in it or its success.

19. *The nonprofit does not understand how to engage in meaningful dialogue.* Discussions in the nonprofit are power plays in which one side wins and one side loses. Strategic planning is a waste of time without ground rules for discussions and deliberations.

20. *Conflict is not dealt with in a healthy fashion.* Perhaps conflict has become so unhealthy that it is creating a dysfunctional organization. If conflict within the organization has become so toxic that it is affecting operations, it needs to be resolved before any meaningful strategic planning can take place.

21. *The nonprofit's board and executive leadership do not understand the concept of organizational systems and the interdependence of these systems, nor do they understand how to change organizational culture and systems processes.* Strategic plans will work only if the strategic planners understand how to introduce lasting change within the organization.

22. *The nonprofit's founder is a dominant force within the organization.* Founder syndrome can also be a barrier to real and lasting change. If the nonprofit's founder is still active within the nonprofit, the person's presence and influence could derail effective strategic planning.

23. *The nonprofit does not understand systems thinking.* Every organization is comprised of systems that interact with each other. Effective strategic planners understand how the organization is structured, what systems are in place, what systems need to be put in place, and how the systems interact and depend on each other.

24. *The nonprofit does not understand how to go about introducing substantive and long-lasting change to the organization.* Strategic planning will not work unless the strategic planners understand what kinds of change need to

be introduced and why the change is essential to achieving strategic goals.

25. *The nonprofit does not see the connection between internal controls and the healthy working of organizational subsystems.* Nonprofits that do not have good internal controls will have difficulty executing a strategic plan.

26. *No one has has any idea what to do next.* Once the strategic plan is written, it is often difficult to determine what to do next. Without specific action steps outlined, the plan will gather dust.

27. *The nonprofit has no idea what the structure of the strategic plan should look like or how to go about articulating the vision for the organization and creating a road map to get there.* If the nonprofit has no idea how even to begin strategic planning, then nothing will happen.

28. *The nonprofit is not in touch with who it is.* Virtually all nonprofits have a mission; some have a vision. However, an essential prerequisite to strategic planning is that the nonprofit understand its organizational culture and problem-solving paradigms.

29. *The nonprofit has no idea whether, as an institution, it will be needed by society in 5 years, 10 years, or longer or how it would need to change to meet the community's needs.* Strategic planning is a waste of time if your nonprofit has no clue as to whether it will be in business in 5 years.

30. *Paralysis by analysis.* Last but not least, if a nonprofit cannot move along in its strategic planning deliberations, there will be no strategic plan.

Why Strategic Plans Are Routinely Ignored after They Are Created—An Analysis of Missed Opportunities

Even if the nonprofit actually does draft a strategic plan, there is no guarantee that it will achieve the intended results. If the contents of the strategic plan are meaningless to everyone except the planning team, then the plan will likely be put on a shelf.

The plan will not succeed if is treated as a top-secret document. Nonprofits are often reluctant to share the contents of the strategic plan, particularly if it contains recommendations for change that would mean consolidation, layoffs, or other measures that would not meet with the approval of the rank and file. In some nonprofits, it would be easier for the staff and volunteers to obtain Osama bin Laden's cell phone number than it would be to obtain a copy of the strategic plan.

Similarly, if no one understands why strategic plans are created, then the plan will likely be ignored. When there is no connection between the plan and the organization's daily operations, the plan will soon be history. By creating a strategic plan that is ignored, the organization has missed the opportunity to use the strategic planning process to examine the entire organization on a systemic level. Even after the strategic plan is written, people still don't know where the organization is headed and what's expected of them.

If the strategic planning process glosses over long-standing problems, then the plan is doomed to failure. No organization is perfect, but sometimes the level of dysfunction within a nonprofit can reach a level that actively interferes with operations and planning.

WHAT DOES ENGAGING IN STRATEGIC PLANNING *ACTUALLY DO* FOR YOUR NONPROFIT?

Engaging in strategic planning brings benefits beyond the creation of the plan itself. Strategic planning forces planners to:

- Look at the nonprofit as it is now for the purpose of envisioning how it can improve.

- Acknowledge that the organization operates in a competitive environment and examine what other nonprofits are competitors.

- Look at how the legal and legislative environments have changed over at least the last five years.

- Examine who your nonprofit is and who it does and does not serve. It's okay if your nonprofit doesn't serve everyone as long as the reasons are clear.

- Think about where the nonprofit needs to go and why.

- Examine whether the nonprofit has the right people on board to achieve strategic goals.

- Examine the nonprofit's organizational systems and the way the nonprofit solves problems. Strategic planning even forces the planners to look at how long it takes for the organization to decide there even *is* a problem.

- Take a look at the nonprofit's culture including the stories that insiders tell about the organization and the stories newcomers hear. Crafts Organizational culture shapes the way in which things get done or the excuses for why things don't get done.

Strategic Planning Does Not Need to Take Forever!

You can prepare a strategic plan for your nonprofit in approximately four weeks. The secret is to invest at least a month in the implementation of Sarbanes-Oxley (SOX) requirements and best practices. The investment of four weeks for SOX implementation and four weeks for strategic planning will reap significant benefits for your nonprofit.

Next Steps

Chapter 2 will present a short history of Sarbanes-Oxley legislation and also describe how legislators at the federal and state levels are addressing nonprofit accountability issues.

Chapter 3 will present an overview of Sarbanes-Oxley requirements and best practices.

Chapter 4 will describe how your nonprofit can utilize a streamlined approach to implement these requirements and best practices.

Chapter 5 will show your nonprofit how to get in touch with its authentic organization. Learning about how your nonprofit actually works is central to writing an effective strategic plan.

Chapter 6 will present an overview of the process of writing a strategic plan.

Chapter 7 will introduce a strategic planning template and timeline to help your nonprofit write an effective strategic plan and take action to achieve your strategic goals.

Chapter 8 will describe how your nonprofit can leverage its SOX compliance and strategic plan to add greater value to the organization.

Chapter 9 will focus on helping small nonprofits scale their SOX compliance and strategic planning efforts to fit the size of their organizations.

The appendices contain worksheets and samples to help your nonprofit create the types of policies and procedures needed for SOX compliance and strategic planning.

This book will change the way your nonprofit thinks about and conducts strategic planning, and will change the way your organization sees the return on investment for your strategic planning dollars.

Sarbanes-Oxley and the New Legislative Environment

INTRODUCTION

In Chapter 1, we discussed the reasons why nonprofits waste so much time, money, and energy attempting to "write" strategic plans. Most of the reasons why nonprofits seem to have such a difficult time doing this type of planning hinge on poorly administered or nonexistent internal controls, management techniques, and understanding about how to actually manage an organization in the twenty-first century.

Many nonprofits have never heard of Sarbanes-Oxley legislation and certainly have no inkling that two of the provisions are required for all organizations regardless of their legal structure. Often, people who have been high-level community volunteers and board members are quick to dismiss the relevance of Sarbanes-Oxley to nonprofit management—particularly if it means they have to change how they are behaving.

The scene is an elegant Minneapolis restaurant. Five career women are having lunch together. Lois is the chief financial officer of a well-known nonprofit in the Twin Cities. Shelly is an attorney with a prominent law firm. Joan is a consultant specializing in nonprofit management. Virginia is a community volunteer who sits on a number of prestigious nonprofit boards. She is also the chair of the board of a historic Minneapolis landmark. The women met for lunch that day because they were colleagues on a *pro bono* project. Joan attempted, once again, to convince Virginia that the conflict of interest presented by a staff member was indeed a serious issue, and the discussion turned to Sarbanes-Oxley. Virginia emphatically stated, "Sarbanes-Oxley has *nothing* to do with nonprofits! You don't know what you are talking about!"

Yes, Virginia, Sarbanes-Oxley does apply to nonprofits!

Sarbanes-Oxley legislation is not simply a set of prescriptive requirements, but a blueprint for establishing a level of order and efficiency within your nonprofit. This level of order and efficiency creates an important momentum that needs to be tapped in order to engage in meaningful strategic planning.

SARBANES-OXLEY LEGISLATION— A BRIEF HISTORY

Where Did This Law Come From?

Sarbanes-Oxley legislation did not simply fall from the sky. The law, officially named "The Public Company Accounting Reform and Investor Protection Act," was passed in 2002 in the wake of the Enron corporate scandal. The act is commonly referred to as the Sarbanes-Oxley Act (SOX), named after Senator Paul Sarbanes (D-MD) and Representative Michael Oxley (R-OH), who were its main sponsors. Both Senator Sarbanes and Representative Oxley retired from Congress in 2006. Although SOX was initially intended to raise the bar for integrity and competence for publicly traded companies (i.e., companies that have stockholders), its effect has been to promote greater accountability within both the nonprofit and private sectors. SOX is the latest in a long progression of regulatory reform aimed at rectifying corporate misdeeds (see Exhibit 2.1).

Why now? Haven't there been corporate scandals in prior decades? The difference between the Enron, MCI, WorldCom, and Arthur Andersen scandals and those that took place in earlier times was the presence and voice of shareholder activists. Although the U.S. market and its investors were stunned by a string of corporate and accounting scandals, the shareholders organized and insisted on accountability and successfully lobbied for tougher laws.

What led up to the Enron implosion was the number of partnership transactions that lost the organization a substantial amount of money. In

EXHIBIT 2.1	SOX LISTING OF TITLES AND SECTIONS

Title	Section
I. Public Company Accounting Oversight Board	101: Establishment, administrative provision 102: Registration with the board 103: Auditing, quality control, and independence standards and rules 104: Inspections of registered public accounting firms 105: Investigations and disciplinary proceedings 106: Foreign public accounting firms 107: Commission oversight of the board 108: Accounting standards 109: Funding
II. Auditor Independence **Best practices for nonprofits come from this section**	201: Services outside the scope of practice of auditors 202: Preapproval requirements 203: Audit partner rotation 204: Auditor reports to audit committees 205: Conforming amendments 206: Conflicts of interest 207: Study of mandatory rotation of registered public accounting firms 208: Commission authority 209: Considerations by appropriate state regulatory authorities
III. Corporate Responsibility **Best practices for nonprofits come from this section**	301: Public company audit committees 302: Corporate responsibility for financial reports 303: Improper influence on conduct of audits 304: Forfeiture of certain bonuses and profits 305: Officer and director bars and penalties 306: Insider trades during pension fund blackout periods 307: Rules of professional responsibility for attorneys 308: Fair funds for investors
IV. Enhanced Financial Disclosures **Best practices for nonprofits come from this section**	401: Disclosures in periodic reports 402: Enhanced conflict-of-interest provisions 403: Disclosure of transactions involving management and principal stockholders 404: Management assessment of internal controls 405: Exemption 406: Code of ethics for senior financial officers

(continued)

EXHIBIT 2.1   (CONTINUED)

Title	Section
	407: Disclosure of audit committee financial expert
	408: Enhanced review of periodic disclosures by issuers
	409: Real-time issuer disclosures
VIII. Corporate and Criminal Fraud Accountability Document preservation Whistle-Blower protection **Best practices for nonprofits come from this section, AND Sections 802 and 806 (document preservation and whistle-blower protection) are legal requirements for ALL organizations, including nonprofits!**	801: Short title 802: Criminal penalties for altering documents 803: Debts nondischareable if incurred in violation of securities fraud laws 804: Statue of limitations for securities fraud 805: Review of federal sentencing guidelines for obstruction of justice and extensive criminal fraud 806: Protection for employees of publicly traded companies who provide evidence of fraud 807: Criminal penalties for defrauding shareholders of publicly traded companies
IX. White-Collar Crime Penalty **Best practices for nonprofits come from this section**	901: Short title 902: Attempts and conspiracies to commit criminal fraud offenses 903: Criminal penalties for mail and wire fraud 904: Criminal penalties for violations of the Employee Retirement Income Security Act of 1974 905: Amendment to sentencing guidelines relating to certain white-collar offenses 906: Corporate responsibility for financial reports
XI. Corporate Fraud and Accountability **Best practices for nonprofits come from this section AND Section 1107 (retaliation against informants) is a legal requirement for ALL organizations, including nonprofits!**	1101: Short title 1102: Tampering with a record or otherwise impeding an official proceeding 1103: Temporary freeze authority for the Securities and Exchange Commission 1104: Amendment to the Federal Sentencing Guidelines 1105: Authority of the Commission to prohibit persons from serving as officers or directors 1106: Increased criminal penalties under Securities Exchange Act of 1934 1107: Retaliation against informants

2001, Enron reported that it had failed to follow generally accepted accounting practices in its financial statements for 1997 through 2001 by excluding these unprofitable transactions. In these erroneous financial statements, the organization reported large profits when, in fact, it had lost a total of $586 million during those years. Neither internal nor external controls "detected" the financial losses disguised as profits—nor did their auditors, Arthur Andersen, because the giant accounting firm had numerous contracts with Enron for auditing services, consulting, accounting services, and the like. Although Enron promptly fired any whistle-blowers, ultimately the revelation of the erroneous financial reporting led to a collapse in the price of Enron stock. The price of Enron stock fell from $83 per share in December 2000 to less than $1 per share in December 2001. However, some of Enron's managers made millions of dollars by selling their company stock before its price plummeted. Other investors experienced substantial losses, including Enron employees who had invested a large portion of their retirement portfolios in Enron stock. Enron employees were prohibited by the company from selling any of their stock as the price plummeted.

Role of Arthur Andersen

The CPA firm of Arthur Andersen, which had been one of the largest accounting firms in the world, served as Enron's auditor throughout the years of erroneous statements. The firm allegedly "overlooked" Enron's questionable accounting practices since it was making a large amount of money for providing Enron with consulting services and did not want to lose the consulting business. The firm was indicted by the U.S. Department of Justice and in 2002 Arthur Andersen LLP was convicted of obstructing justice by shredding Enron-related documents requested by the Securities and Exchange Commission (SEC). The corporation subsequently folded as all of its corporate clients withdrew their accounts. Andersen's role in the Enron scandal is reflected in the SOX requirements to ensure auditor independence.[1]

What should be noteworthy to all nonprofit readers is that an auditor is either independent or not. Many nonprofits are reluctant to find a truly independent auditor because it would cost more money and they are able to obtain other services from their current auditor. *You can't have it both ways!*

How Has the Legislative Environment Changed for Nonprofits?

Why SOX Compliance Is Here to Stay

Sarbanes–Oxley compliance is *not* a fad that is going away. Senator Max Baucus (D–MT), chair of the Senate Finance Committee and his Republican counterpart, Charles Grassley (R–IA) have worked on nonprofit account-ability in a collaborative fashion that is quite exceptional by Capitol Hill standards. Both senators are committed to nonprofit accountability and believe that the time has come to implement a level of accountability and transparency by law and regulation to nonprofit management and govern-ance. To that end, they held hearings on nonprofit accountability in 2004 and 2005 when Senator Grassley was the chair of the Finance Committee. As part of the Senate Finance Committee's June 2004 and April 2005 hearings on nonprofit accountability, Mark W. Everson, the commissioner of the Internal Revenue Service (IRS), provided some very sobering testimony on that agency's plans for oversight and enforcement of the nonprofit sector.

Summary of IRS Commissioner's Testimony at the 2004 and 2005 Grassley Hearings

Commissioner Everson testified that the Bush administration is committed to supporting the IRS's more aggressive oversight and enforcement rules related to nonprofit organizations.[2] The IRS's short-term agenda for bringing about nonprofit accountability includes:

- *Addressing the scope of the abuses of tax advantages.* "The approximately 3 million tax-exempt entities include almost 1 million section 501(c)(3) charities and almost 1 million employee plans. This sector is a vital part of our nation's economy that employs about one in every four workers in the United States. In addition, nearly one-fifth of the total U.S. securities market is held by employee plans alone. There are abuses of charities that principally rely on the tax advantages conferred by the deductibility of contributions to those organizations. If these abuses are left unchecked, I believe there is the risk that Americans not only will lose faith in and reduce support for charitable organizations, but that the integrity of our tax system also will be compromised. I am committed to combating abuse in this area."

What does this mean for nonprofits? The IRS is committed to aggressive oversight of nonprofit operations so that current and potential donors do not lose faith in the system.

- *Scope of the IRS strategic plan for 2005–2009.* "Along with improving service and modernizing computer systems, one of the strategic goals is to enhance enforcement of the tax law. . . . Historically, IRS functions regulating tax-exempt entities have not been well funded due to the lack of revenue they generated. This view is misdirected in light of the size and importance of the sector. With staffing in this area flat at best and with the number of charities increasing annually, our audit coverage has fallen to historically low levels, compromising our ability to maintain an effective enforcement presence in the exempt organizations community. One of the plan's four specific objectives is to deter abuse within tax-exempt and governmental entities, and misuse of these entities by third parties for tax avoidance or other unintended purposes. . . . Despite the importance of this sector, until recently our enforcement budget was not keeping up with its growth. By September [2005] we will see a 30 percent increase in enforcement personnel for exempt organizations over September 2003 levels."

What does this mean for nonprofits? The Bush administration has allocated additional funding and staff to the IRS to enforce the law and prosecute nonprofits and individuals who use tax-exempt entities to avoid paying taxes. This comment was primarily aimed at wealthy individuals who use designated donations to foundations as a means of avoiding taxes.

- *Filing of Form 990.*— "The IRS will be looking at organizations that failed to or did not fully complete compensation information on Form 990. This information will help inform the IRS about current practices of self-governance, both best practices and compliance gaps, and will help the agency focus our examination program to address specific problem areas."

What does this mean for nonprofits? The IRS expects your nonprofit to file an IRS Form 990 every year—without exception. They have instituted an online "e-filing" to facilitate this process. The IRS filing should be complete, accurate, and *provide all of the information requested*. For example, your nonprofit's 990 would disclose how much money was raised in fund-raising activities. The 990 must also *accurately* disclose the level of expenses that were incurred to raise the funds.

- *Enhancing nonprofit governance.* "Stronger governance procedures are needed for exempt organizations. The sanctions for serious lapses in governance are clear. There is the possibility of revocation of exemption, along with the various excise taxes against individuals that I mentioned before. But sanctions are a last resort . . . organizations without effective governance controls are more likely to have compliance problems. . . . [*The IRS will*] require disclosure of whether the organization has a conflict-of-interest policy or an independent audit committee, and whether additional disclosure should be required concerning certain financial transactions or insider relationships. . . . Our Form 990 revision team is working on a comprehensive overhaul of the form to provide better compliance information about these organizations to the IRS, the states, and the public. . . .

What does this mean for nonprofits?   The IRS is committed to ensuring that nonprofits are governed by a competent board that has a conflict-of-interest policy and independent audit committee. The IRS has a Form 990 revision team that is working to modify the current IRS 990 to require nonprofits to disclose their compliance with these stipulations.

- *The administration strongly encourages and supports donations to our charities.* "Some entities now use their privileged status to achieve ends that Congress never imagined when it conferred tax exemption."

What does this mean for nonprofits?   The IRS will more aggressively enforce the regulations around obtaining and keeping an IRS 501(c)(3) designation.

- *Nonprofit compliance issues.* "A number of factors are impacting compliance in the tax-exempt area. As might be expected, these factors do not necessarily operate independently of one another. Taken together, however, they add up to a *culture that has become more casual about compliance and less resistant to noncompliance*. These are attitudes that we must work together to change."

What does this mean for nonprofits? The IRS commissioner was politely pointing out that the nonprofit world has traditionally been allowed to do as it pleased without any legislative or regulatory oversight. He is also pointing out that the current rash of nonprofit scandals should bring this leniency to a halt. The IRS is as committed as the Senate Finance Committee is to forcing compliance within the nonprofit sector.

- *Lax attitudes toward governance.* "An independent, empowered, and active board of directors is the key to ensuring that a tax-exempt organization serves public purposes and does not misuse or squander the resources in its trust. Unfortunately, the nonprofit community has not been immune from recent trends toward bad corporate practices. Like their for-profit brethren, many charitable boards appear to be lax in certain areas. Many of the situations in which we have found otherwise law-abiding organizations to be off-track stem from the failure of fiduciaries to appropriately manage the organization . . . We have found issues relating to how executive compensation is set and reported by nonprofits. Similarly, issues exist as to whether sufficient due diligence and care is taken in filing tax and information returns."

What does this mean for nonprofits? The IRS has found that many of the nonprofits that were involved in scandals had boards that were not behaving in a manner consistent with their legal obligations. In other words, they were clueless about what their obligations were and not particularly interested in engaging in responsible governance. The IRS has also found that those nonprofits whose executives received excessive compensation generally were able to arrange for the compensation without any oversight from the board. All of this means that the IRS will be reviewing IRS 990s much more diligently.

- *Improved transparency in the tax-exempt sector.* "A positive development in recent years is the improvement in 'transparency' within the tax-exempt sector. The use of the term *transparency* refers to the ability of outsiders—donors, the press, interested members of the public—to review data concerning the finances and operations of a tax-exempt organization. By creating a means by which the public may review and monitor the activities of tax-exempt organizations, we promote compliance, help preserve the integrity of the tax system, and help maintain public confidence in the charitable sector. To achieve these goals, we began in the mid-to-late 1990s to image Forms 990, the annual information returns filed by many tax-exempt organizations. We put this information on CDs, and provide it to members of the public, including a number of watchdog groups that monitor charitable organizations. These groups put the information up on their web sites, where it is available to the press and to the public. This process has resulted in increased press and public scrutiny of the tax-exempt sector, which we believe is highly desirable. It has also increased the ability of the IRS and state regulators to access Form 990 data, because they are more readily available. Transparency is a linchpin of compliance within the sector. Therefore, part of our work is to improve exempt organization transparency, including better data quality and better data availability. . . . Under proposed and temporary regulations, by 2007 we will require electronic filing for larger public charities and all private foundations."

What does this mean for nonprofits?   The focus on increasing transparency centers on making the IRS 990 filings readily available on CDs or the Internet or on nonprofit web sites. This emphasis on transparency also means that the IRS expects the nonprofit's 990 to be accurate and complete.

Senate Finance Committee: Grassley White Paper

Subsequent to the 2004 hearings and testimony, a staff discussion paper was released with recommendations for closer regulation of nonprofits. These are simply a series of recommendations made by the congressional staff at that time, but the tone and reach of the recommendations should be taken seriously by every nonprofit regardless of size.

The preface to the document instructs the reader that "The document reflects proposals for reforms and best practices in the area of tax-exempt organizations based on staff investigations and research as well as proposals from practitioners, officers and directors of charities, academia and other interested parties. This document is a work-in-progress and is meant to encourage and foster additional comments and suggestions as the Finance Committee continues to consider possible legislation."[3]

The White Paper is a set of suggestions prepared at the request of the then-chairman of the Senate Finance Committee, Senator Charles

Grassley (R-IA). This Committee's stance on nonprofits, however, is unlikely to change with the shift in party majority as Senators Baucus and Grassley appeared to share the same perspective on nonprofit accountability. The following recommendations could very well be implemented in the wake of any future scandals of the magnitude of the United Way or Red Cross. An unfortunate characteristic of nonprofit scandals is the Velcro effect on the rest of the sector.[4]

Some of the proposals in the 2004 White Paper include:

- *A five-year review of tax-exempt status of every nonprofit by the IRS.* On every fifth anniversary of the IRS's determination of the tax-exempt status of an organization that is required to apply for such status, the organization would be required to file with the IRS such information as would *enable the IRS to determine whether the organization continues to be organized and operated exclusively for a exempt purposes* (i.e., whether the original determination letter should remain in effect). Information to be filed would include current articles of incorporation and bylaws, conflict-of-interest policies, evidence of accreditation, management policies regarding best practices, a detailed narrative about the organization's practices, and financial statements

What does this mean for nonprofits? This recommendation would require nonprofits to submit documentation every five years that proves to the IRS that the organization continues to be in compliance with its 501 (c)(3) designation. The list of documents specified below is particularly enlightening about the intent of this proposal:

- *Current articles of incorporation and bylaws.* The nonprofit would need to be clear about how their operations and governance continues to be in harmony with its founding documents.

- *Conflict-of-interest policies.* The nonprofit would have to provide evidence of a conflict-of-interest policy and, most likely, proof that board members and senior management have completed annual affidavits identifying real or potential conflicts of interest.

- *Evidence of accreditation.* This document would be based on another recommendation, which is that nonprofits be required to obtain specific accreditation. (This recommendation is discussed later in this section.)

- *Management policies regarding best practices.* The nonprofit would be required to develop and submit written policies that demonstrate that the organization is implementing best practices in management and governance.

- *A detailed narrative about the organization's practices.* This document would require the nonprofit to provide a detailed explanation about what the organization does and why it is necessary/desirable in the community.

- *Financial statements.* These financial statements would be supplemental to the Form 990 that is required on an annual basis.

Form 990—Proposals for Reform

The White Paper recommends that nonprofits improve the quality and scope of Form 990 and financial statements. This recommendation is consistent with the IRS commissioner's testimony at the Grassley hearings in 2004 and 2005. The White Paper noted that in a report to the Finance Committee, the General Accounting Office found significant problems in the accuracy and completeness of Form 990. Other studies have highlighted that there are no common standards for filing Form 990, and thus similarly situated charities can have very different Forms 990.

Some other recommendations about Form 990 reforms include:

- *Form 990s would require signature by chief executive officer (CEO).* The CEO (or equivalent officer) of a tax-exempt organization would be required to sign a declaration under penalties of perjury that he or she has put in place processes and procedures to ensure that the organization's federal information return and tax return (including Form 990T) complies with the Internal Revenue Code and that the CEO was provided reasonable assurance of the accuracy and completeness of all material aspects of the return. This declaration would be part of the information or tax return. The recommendation clearly states that nonprofit executives and board members should be held to the same criminal liability standards as those of their private-sector counterparts. Bringing the expectations of nonprofit accountability in line with expectations for private-sector accountability is a recurring theme in today's legal environment.

- *Penalties for failure to file a complete and accurate Form 990.* The present penalty for failure to file or to include required information is $20 per day up to the lesser of $10,000 or 5 percent of gross receipts per return (increased to $100 per day up to $50,000 per return for organizations with gross receipts over $1 million in a year). Under the proposal, the penalty for failure to file would be doubled and for organizations with gross receipts over $2 million per year; the present penalty would be tripled. Failure to file a required 990 for two consecutive years (or for three of four years) could result in loss of tax exemption or other penalties, such as loss of status as an organization to which deductible contributions may be made.

  As Commissioner Everson stated, the IRS has stepped up surveillance and enforcement of nonprofit compliance with respect to filing Form 990. The reality of penalties for failing to file a Form 990 is already here. Although the White Paper recommends loss of tax exemption, the reality is that the IRS is already taking action against nonprofits that do not file Form 990 on an annual basis. For a nonprofit, this means the organization can no longer tell donors that their contributions are tax exempt. In other words, the "nonprofit" is out of business.

- *Required disclosure of performance goals, activities, and expenses in Form 990 and financial statements.* The White Paper recommends that charitable organizations with over $250,000 in gross receipts would be required to include in the Form 990 a detailed description of the organization's annual performance goals and measurements for meeting those goals (to be established by the board of directors) for the past year and goals for the coming year. The purpose of this requirement would be to assist donors to better determine an organization's accomplishments and goals in deciding whether to donate, and not as a point of review by the IRS. Charitable organizations would be required to disclose material changes in activities, operations, or structure as well as to accurately report the charity's expenses, including any joint cost allocations, in its financial statements and Form 990.

  Transparency is the predominant theme of these recommendations. The volume of public complaints about nonprofit organizations was undoubtedly the catalyst behind these recommendations. In recent years, the media has conducted many investigations of bogus charities, and certainly some charities that are "household names" have also abused donor trust by misdirecting donations to exorbitant salaries, expenses, and so on. The continuing criticism of post-Katrina response by the Red Cross is an example of how public donations have not been allocated in a manner anticipated by the donors.

- *Nonprofits would be required to make certain documents publicly available.* This recommendation is already in place as all nonprofits are required to provide a copy of their latest Form 990 to anyone requesting the document. For charitable organizations, public oversight provides donors with vital information for determining which organizations have the programs and practices that will ensure that contributions will be spent as intended. Exempt organizations with a web site would be required to post on such site any return that is required to be made public by present law, the organization's application for tax exemption, the organization's determination letter from the IRS, and the organization's financial statements for the five most recent years.

The recommendations are, again, aimed at ensuring that the public has access to information that would be vital to their making a decision to make a donation. Of particular note is the recommendation that the nonprofit's web site be employed to present not only those documents currently required (Form 990) but also:

- The organization's application for tax exemption
- The organization's determination letter from the IRS
- The organization's financial statements from the five most recent years

State Laws and Nonprofit Accountability

Presently, California is the only state with a nonprofit accountability law, the Nonprofit Integrity Act (SB1262).[5] The law was nicknamed the "Sarbanes-Oxley clone" for nonprofits. It is important to note that this law applies not only to those nonprofits *domiciled* in California, *but to any nonprofit, regardless of where they are domiciled, that solicits donations in the state of California.* This law was initiated by the then attorney general, William Lockyer, because of the volume of complaints his office was receiving from the public. Again, just as shareholder activism was the catalyst for the passage of the Sarbanes-Oxley legislation, the public's outrage at nonprofit malfeasance provided the catalyst for a similar class of legislation.

Provisions that Apply to Nonprofits with Budgets in Excess of $2 Million

The Nonprofit Integrity Act imposes many of the features of Sarbanes-Oxley legislation on nonprofits with budgets in excess of $2 million operating in California.

Key provisions of this law include:

- Nonprofits will be required to have an annual audit performed by a certified public accountant (CPA) who is "independent" as defined by U.S. government auditing standards.

- The results of the audit will need to be made available to the public and the attorney general.

- Nonprofits will be required to have an audit committee whose membership cannot include staff and must not overlap more than 50 percent with the finance committee; the audit committee can include members who are not on the organization's board of directors.

What does this mean for nonprofits in California? To ensure greater accountability in executive compensation, the law requires that the board approve the compensation, including benefits, of the corporation's president or CEO, and its treasurer or chief financial officer (CFO), for the purposes of assuring that these executives' compensation package is reasonable.

What else does this mean for nonprofits in California? The law requires disclosure of written contracts between commercial fund-raisers and nonprofits, which must be available for review on demand from the attorney general's office. Fund-raisers must be registered with the attorney general's office.

The following points in the law apply to all nonprofits, regardless of size, in California:

- The law expects nonprofits to make their audits available to the public on the same basis as their IRS Form 990 if they prepare financial statements that are audited by a CPA.

- Except for emergencies, notice of a solicitation campaign by a "commercial fund-raiser for charitable purposes" must be filed at least 10 days before the commencement of the solicitation campaign, events, or other services. Each contract must be signed by an official of the nonprofit, and include the contract provisions specified in the law.

- Regarding fund-raising activities, the law states that nonprofits must not misrepresent or mislead anyone about its purpose, or the nature, purpose, or beneficiary of a solicitation. Further, the law specifies that there be specific disclosures in any solicitation that the funds raised will be used for the charitable purpose as expressed in articles of incorporation or other governing documents. The nonprofit is expected to ensure that fund-raising activities are adequately supervised to ensure that contracts and agreements are in order and that fund-raising is conducted without intimidation or undue influence.[6]

What does this mean for nonprofits in California? Nonprofits in California, regardless of their size, need to review their fund-raising practices, particularly if some or all of their fund-raising is outsourced to commercial fund-raising firms. Nonprofits will be liable for abuses by vendors of fund-raising services. As a practical matter, boards should insist that due diligence activities be conducted before contracting with any vendor, particularly those providing fund-raising services. The California law, however, places strict parameters around third-party fund-raising.[7]

So What Are the Sarbanes-Oxley Requirements and Best Practices for Nonprofits?

Currently, only a few of the provisions in SOX directly apply to nonprofit organizations. Nonprofits are required to adhere to Title III, Section 806, and Title XI, Section 1107, which provide protection to employees who report suspected fraud or other illegal activities. In addition, Title VIII, Section 802, and Title XI, Section 1102, which address the destruction or falsification of records or documents, apply to nonprofits.[8]

The nonprofit sector has recently experienced its own recent scandals of perceived wrongdoing and fiscal mismanagement. For example, the United Way and the American Red Cross have received substantial unfavorable media coverage of their apparent failures in accountability and adherence to mission.[9] Incidents such as these have cast the nonprofit sector in an unfavorable light, and have damaged the public's trust in the integrity and the public benefit of nonprofits. While it is true that the majority of the SOX provisions currently apply only to publicly traded corporations and not to nonprofit organizations, nonprofits could benefit operationally from adopting some of the SOX rules as best practices. In addition, voluntarily adhering to the SOX "gold standards" would create greater credibility and ability to recruit high-quality board members, as well as attracting the favorable attention of major donors, foundations, and other funding sources.

Sox Requirements for all Organizations—Even Nonprofits!

Whistle-Blower Protection

The first obligation from SOX that applies to all organizations is the requirement for a documented whistle-blower protection policy. SOX requires all organizations, including nonprofits, to establish a means to collect, retain, and resolve claims regarding accounting, internal accounting controls, and auditing matters. The system must allow for such concerns to be submitted anonymously. SOX provides significant protections to whistle-blowers, and severe penalties to those that retaliate against them.[10]

Chapter 4 will describe how your nonprofit can institute a whistle-blower protection policy that has these features:

- There is a confidential avenue for reporting suspected waste, fraud, and abuse.
- There is a process to thoroughly investigate any reports.
- There is a process for disseminating the findings from the investigation.
- The employee filing the complaint will not be subjected to termination, firing, or harassment, or miss out on promotion.
- Even if the findings do not support the nature of the complaint, the employee or volunteer who made the complaint will not face any repercussions.

All employees and volunteers should have a copy of the whistle-blower policy and it should be posted in clear view. This policy should also be covered in any orientation or training programs the organization offers for its employees and volunteers.

Document Management and Preservation Policy

Document storage and retention is another area within SOX that applies to all organizations. All organizations must have a method for storing and archiving documents and a specific prohibition against destroying document if the nonprofit is under investigation or involved in legal action.[11] Chapter 4 presents a streamlined method for your nonprofit to implement a document preservation policy for paper and electronic files.

SOX Best Practices

SOX best practices are designed to enhance the completeness and reliability of all aspects of your nonprofit's operations. These practices are:

- Establishment of an audit committee whose role is to oversee the annual audit or financial review (for small nonprofits) and to upgrade the financial literacy of the board
- Enhanced detail and accuracy in the preparation of IRS Form 990
- Improved governance and a nonprofit board that understands its role as ultimately accountable for the actions of the nonprofit, and is willing to take steps to enhance professional development for each member
- Conflict-of-interest policy and code of ethics, which facilitates greater focus on decision making for the good of the nonprofit
- Internal controls, particularly as these relate to financial operations, and compliance with all laws and regulations at the federal, state, and local level
- Transparency at all levels of management
- Adherence to policies and procedures—and enforcement

Implementing these best practices will help your nonprofit establish the types of management practices that are considered to be the gold standard in the corporate and nonprofit worlds. These best practices will also add value to your nonprofit because they will result in a higher level of management and staff accountability and a more effective board whose members understand and adhere to their fiduciary obligations and recognize their responsibility in governing the company. The best practices will also create effective protocols to ensure that the company remains in compliance with SOX and the company's "industry standards" and addresses future standards. Your nonprofit's marketing efforts will be improved because the best practices will set you apart from most nonprofits. The result is better competitive positioning by making known that the nonprofit adheres to the SOX gold standard in its operating practices.

Implementing the best practices will also pay dividends in your nonprofit's strategic planning because your nonprofit will gain greater credibility and ability to attract necessary resources, be these in the form of high-quality board members, sources of capital, donors, or other fund sources.

NEXT STEPS

Chapter 3 will provide an overview of whistle-blower protection, document preservation and best practices. Chapter 4 will describe the streamline approaches that will assist you in implementing these valuable policies and procedures.

▮ NOTES

1. Jackson, Peggy M., and Toni E. Fogarty. 2006. *Sarbanes-Oxley and Nonprofit Management.* Hoboken, N.J.: John Wiley & Sons, pp. 17–21.
2. Everson, Mark W., Commissioner of the Internal Revenue Service. 2005. Testimony before the U.S. Senate Finance Committee hearings on *Charity Oversight and Reform: Keeping Bad Things from Happening to Good Charities,* Washington, D.C., June 2004; and Testimony before the U.S. Senate Finance Committee hearings on Charities and Charitable Giving: Proposals for Reform. Washington, D.C., April.
3. United States Senate Finance Committee. 2004. Staff Discussion Paper released in conjunction with June 2004 hearings on *Charity Oversight and Reform: Keeping Bad Things from Happening to Good Charities.* Washington, D.C., June.
4. The term *Velcro effect* described the lasting implications of nonprofit corporate scandal on the sector at large. Light, Paul C. 2004. *Fact Sheet on the Continued Crisis in Charitable Confidence.* Washington, D.C.: Brookings Institution, September 13.
5. Larsen, K. 2004. "Summary: SB1262 'The Nonprofit Integrity Act,'" California Association of Nonprofits, retrieved on March 1, 2005 from http://www2.niac.

org/Documents/DocumentRetrieve.cfm?q_DocumentID=147&UploadDocClass=DynamicContent.

6. Id.

7. Nonprofit Integrity Act (2004), State of California, State Senate Bill 1262, September 2004.

8. Public Company Accounting Reform and Investor Protection Act of 2002, H.R. 3763, 107th Congress, P.L. 107–204, retrieved on January 28, 2004, from http://frwebgate.access. gpo.gov/cgi-bin/getdoc.cgi?dbname=107_cong_public_laws&docid=f:publ204.107.

9. *Chronicle of Philanthropy.* 2004. "Ex-United Way CEO Gets Jail Sentence," retrieved May 23, 2005 from http://www.unitedwaynca.org/website/content/media/pdf/chronphil5-27-04.pdf.

   Grassley, Charles. 2002. Letter to Marsha Evans. Washington, D.C., August 12.

10. See note 8.

11. Id.

Introduction to SOX Compliance and Best Practices

INTRODUCTION

In this chapter we will discuss the two provisions of the law that are required for all organizations whether they are publicly traded, private, or nonprofit. We will also discuss the best practices that have emerged from the implementation of the law. The implementation of SOX requirements and best practices contain important benefits to the quality of your nonprofit's management and to the efficiency and cost-effectiveness of its operations.

WHAT ARE THE SOX REQUIREMENTS AND BEST PRACTICES?

As discussed in Chapter 2, currently, only two of the provisions in SOX directly apply to nonprofit organizations—whistle-blower protection and document preservation. Nonprofits are required to adhere to whistle-blower protection requirements that provide protection to employees who report suspected fraud or other illegal activities. Employees or volunteers of a nonprofit are shielded from retaliation for making reports of waste, fraud, or abuse. Nonprofits are also expected to have a fully functioning document preservation policy in place. The document preservation policy has two aspects: preservation and archiving of documents for the purpose of timely retrieval, and a prohibition against the destruction or falsification of records or documents. Ironically, both Enron and Arthur Andersen were ultimately brought down because they shredded or attempted to shred important evidence. Their actions were so egregious that Congress made sure to include the provision that documents that were material to an investigation and/or legal proceedings were prohibited from being destroyed.[1]

Whistle-Blower Protection

The first obligation from SOX that applies to all organizations is the requirement for a documented whistle-blower protection policy. SOX requires all organizations, including nonprofits, to establish a means to collect, retain, and resolve claims regarding accounting, internal accounting controls, and auditing matters. The system must allow such concerns to be submitted anonymously. SOX provides significant protections to whistle-blowers, and severe penalties to those who retaliate against them. Policies and procedures on whistle-blower protection should contain at least the following features:

- There is a confidential avenue for reporting suspected waste, fraud, and abuse.
- There is a process to thoroughly investigate any reports.
- There is a process for disseminating the findings from the investigation.
- The employee filing the complaint will not be subjected to termination, firing, harassment, or miss out on promotion.
- Even if the findings do not support the nature of the complaint, the employee or volunteer who made the complaint will not face any repercussions.
- All employees and volunteers should have a copy of the whistle-blower policy and it should be posted in clear view. This policy should also be covered in any orientation or training programs the organization offers for its employees and volunteers.

What's the Value of Whistle-Blower Protection?   In the early days of the Industrial Revolution, the demand for coal resulted in the rapid expansion of the mining industry. Because mining is a very dangerous industry, steps were taken that appear to be primitive in today's workplace to reduce the danger for miners. One measure was the carrying of caged canaries in coal mines. As long as the birds remained alive, miners knew that the air was safe to breathe. The canaries were the first indicators that something was amiss—and were invaluable in preventing needless tragedy.

We've come a long way from the Industrial Revolution of the nineteenth century, but workplaces still need to have an early warning system that detects when something is amiss in the management or internal controls of an organization. Whistle-blower protection can be the first line of defense in a nonprofit. If an employee or volunteer is behaving in a manner that is inappropriate, criminal, or creating potential liability, the behavior cannot be ignored. Under Sarbanes-Oxley legislation, the person who makes the report cannot be terminated, harassed, or otherwise punished for bringing the matter to the attention of management.

One of the challenges of implementing a whistle-blower protection policy is that there are common misconceptions about whistle-blowers. *A whistle-blower is not a snitch!* A whistle-blower is someone who is courageous enough to report a situation that has the potential to irreparably harm the organization. Boards and senior management should begin by creating an atmosphere in which whistle-blower protection is not only trumpeted, but whistle-blowers are accorded *hero status*. The whistle-blower could very well be saving your nonprofit from extinction. These people deserve to be rewarded, not reviled!

Whistle-Blower Reports Come in Many Forms: *Pay Attention to Reports of Problems*   There are many ways in which staff, volunteers, or members of a nonprofit organization convey their sentiments or report problems. Some nonprofits solicit feedback via instruments such as surveys or suggestion boxes. Other types of feedback are conveyed without being solicited. The spirit and letter of a whistle-blower protection policy is that feedback or reports, whether solicited or not, will not subject the sender to any negative consequences. The management of a nonprofit organization need not approve of the content of the report or comment, but cannot subject the person making the report or comment to negative consequences.

Consider the results of the survey disseminated by the Riverside Community Federation to evaluate the management quality of the current committee chairs. The survey was voluntary, but all members of the Federation were encouraged to complete it. One member, Molly Compton, completed the survey and commented that the section chair, Mary Smith, was unsatisfactory in her performance. Mary was furious that one of the members dared to criticize her performance and immediately suspected Molly. Mary called Molly and left an irate message on her voice mail insisting that Molly call her back to discuss the comments. Molly sent Mary an e-mail stating that she stood by the comments and refused to discuss it further. Mary continued to send e-mails until Molly threatened to file a formal complaint with the Federation's president.

Moral of the story: If you disseminate a survey, the results are what they are. The nonprofit's management has no right to exact retribution because they don't like someone's response to the survey. Surveys can also be considered a venue for whistle-blowers and are subject to whistle-blower protection.

Whistle-blower protection policies apply to volunteers as well as to paid staff. Volunteer whistle-blowers can observe criminal behavior and should know what the procedures are to report it. Similarly, as in the case of the Riverside Federation, whistle-blower venues can be used to hold volunteer managers accountable for their behavior. Just having a whistle-blower protection policy isn't enough. The Riverside Federation's Mary Smith violated the spirit of whistle-blower protection. Just because your non-profit's board or management doesn't like what they hear, that does not give them the right to mistreat the whistle-blower. Whistle-blower protection needs to be enforced and the nonprofit's leadership needs to be trained to accept all comments and feedback in a manner that is consistent with the spirit and letter of the law. Confidentiality is the key in developing a process whereby employees and volunteers feel safe in reporting waste, fraud, and abuse—or even inferior leadership.

Types of Whistle-Blower Reports   Whistle-blower reports can address a variety of reporting issues, such as:

- Accounting irregularities including unexplained checks, accounts that are not in balance, unauthorized orders and other indicators of mismanagement.

- Violations of governmental regulations, including Occupational Safety and Health Administration (OSHA) regulations, Internal Revenue Service (IRS) regulations, or regulations from state or local governments.

- Fraud can appear in a wide array of transactions. Staff or volunteers who suspect fraud should report it immediately.

- Falsification or destruction of organizational records is another important type of whistle-blower report.

- Possible workplace violence, including reports of threats or menacing behavior, should be reported immediately.

- Discrimination and sexual harassment are whistle-blower reports that are often ignored or repudiated. The whistle-blower policy requires that reports of this type of behavior be investigated immediately.

- Conflicts of interest can be a more subtle type of problem, but if a conflict of interest exists, the problem must be reported.

- Release of proprietary information particularly if the information has been removed from the workplace. In today's world of technology— web blogs, e-mail, and other somewhat anonymous venues—release of proprietary information can be very damaging and should be reported at once.

Chapter 4 presents a method of designing whistle-blower protection policy, including recommendations for talking to your nonprofit's staff and volunteers about fraud. The sooner that a report of waste, fraud, or abuse can be made, the quicker the issue can be addressed. Whistle-blowers are a crucial resource for your nonprofit. They can help you to mitigate a problem before it becomes a crisis.

Document Preservation Policy

Document management and preservation is another area within SOX that applies to all organizations. Every nonprofit has what appears to be too much paper. Managing that paper, as well as electronic files, important e-mail, text messages, and voice mails, is essential to ensuring that the nonprofit meets this SOX requirement. An important part of this requirement is to institute a policy that prohibits destruction of documents during an inquiry or legal action.

Policies on document preservation should be developed by the board and senior management. The nonprofit's executive director should prepare a document that describes what the document preservation policy is and why it is required by law.[2] It is important that the staff and volunteers understand that document preservation is a requirement of SOX that this requirement applies to all businesses and nonprofits.

Chapter 4 presents a streamlined approach to implementing a document preservation policy. Everyone in the nonprofit, from board members to volunteers, needs to understand how it works and how to maintain the system. This means that the system should not be cumbersome and the procedures for maintaining the system should be reasonable. The policy should also clearly describe the new procedures and the results that the nonprofit expects. Expectations of individual performance need to be specified as well as the consequences for failing to adhere to the new procedures.

What are SOX Best Practices?

As SOX legislation has been implemented in corporations throughout the country, important learning has emerged. In addition to the SOX requirements, the nonprofit is expected to implement best practices, which have emerged from the other provisions of the SOX legislation. An array of best practices has emerged from the implementation of the SOX law in the private sector. These best practices have benefits at a number of levels. Although many companies in the private sector have grudgingly implemented the provisions of the law, the subsequent improvement in the overall quality and efficiency of operations has served to reinforce the value of the law.[3]

These best practices include:

- *Internal controls.* Each department within the nonprofit must have a system of internal controls.
- *Adherence to policies and procedures and enforcement.* Once new policies and procedures are in place for SOX compliance, it is important to maintain these practices.
- *Transparency at all levels* of management, including the board.
- *Conflict-of-interest policy,* which facilitates greater focus on decision making for the good of the nonprofit.
- *Code of ethics* for board and senior management that precludes any loans to directors, officers, management, or staff of the nonprofit.
- *Enhanced detail and accuracy in the preparation of IRS tax documents* in the annual submission of IRS 990 filings.

- *Appointing an audit committee* whose role is to oversee the annual audit or financial review (for small nonprofits) and to upgrade the financial literacy of the board.

- *Segregation of auditor's duties.* Auditors must only audit a nonprofit's books and not provide additional services.

- *Certified financial statements.* The nonprofit's board and senior management is ultimately accountable for the accuracy and integrity of the nonprofit's financial statements as well as the nonprofit's IRS 990 forms.

- *Improved governance* and a nonprofit board that understands its role as ultimately accountable for the actions of the nonprofit and is willing to take steps to enhance professional development for each member.

SOX Requirements, Best Practices, and Today's Legislative Environment

The nonprofit world stands to learn a great deal from the private sector in terms of accountability and transparency. As noted in Chapter 2, Congress and state legislatures are intent upon improving the quality of nonprofit management and governance. The implementation of SOX requirements and best practices will directly address a number of areas discussed in Senator Grassley's 2004 and 2005 Finance Committee hearings on nonprofit accountability. To review, these areas include:

- *Ensuring that the nonprofit operations are consistent with its mission and stated purpose presented during its application for its IRS 501(c)(3) designation.* Congress and the IRS are increasing the level of scrutiny that is applied to ensuring that nonprofits are who they say they are and do what they say they are doing.

- *Proper completion and filing of IRS Form 990.* The IRS has prepared extensive materials for nonprofits to review to ensure that Form 990 filings are accurate, complete, and submitted on time every year.

- *Improved governance.* Just as in the private sector, nonprofit boards are under a much higher level of scrutiny and are expected to show leadership in adhering to SOX requirements and best practices.

- *Improved management practices.* SOX best practices have become the gold standard for nonprofit management. Congress and state legislatures, particularly California, have documented their expectations for nonprofit management.

- *Overall accountability and transparency of the nonprofit's board and management to ensure that donor funds are spent in the manner that the donor intended.* This is one of the most important reasons for implementing SOX requirements and best practices. The shareholder activism seen in the corporate world can be seen in the donor activism that served as the catalyst in the quantity and tone of the complaints about nonprofits that are lodged with Congress and the states' attorneys general offices.

Benefits of SOX Implementation: Save Money and Improve Efficiency

Implementation of SOX requirements can save your nonprofit money and improve overall efficiency. By implementing SOX requirements and best practices, your nonprofit can enjoy these benefits:

- *Better interest rates.* Interest rates on loans are based on the lender's perception of risk. Being in compliance with SOX requirements and implementing the best practices that emerged from the SOX legislation will help your nonprofit improve its credit rating and demonstrate that it is a better credit risk.

- *More competitive terms for loans or lines of credit.* As your nonprofit adopts SOX requirements and best practices, these efforts could have a positive effect on the nonprofit's credit rating. Additionally, being able to demonstrate that your nonprofit is in compliance could be beneficial in negotiating the terms of a loan or line of credit

- *Positions your nonprofit to negotiate a more favorable fee from auditors.* Although there has been significant media coverage on increasing costs of audits, much of these fee increases have been because auditors' client organizations are not in compliance. If you feel that your auditor's fees are too high, bid out the job! Don't settle for less than complete value for your auditing dollar. Consider using smaller accounting nonprofits, but don't let them talk you into having them provide services beyond auditing. Ensure that you supply information on your nonprofit's compliance practices to prospective auditors and aggressively negotiate the fees.

- *Positions your nonprofit to obtain insurance coverage at more a competitive premium.* Insurance underwriters are highly reluctant to extend coverage to businesses that are not in compliance. Because SOX compliance is today's gold standard for management, underwriters are looking for evidence that your nonprofit has taken the initiative to integrate SOX requirements and best practices into your day-to-day operations. That tells the underwriter that you know what you are doing and are serious about maintaining a well-run nonprofit.

- *Create additional value from the relationships* that your nonprofit already has with its bank, legal counsel, insurance professional, and information technology (IT) professional. Bringing your nonprofit into compliance can be facilitated by discussions with these people. They should know your nonprofit's business inside-out. If they don't, then you need to seriously consider finding advisers who can meet these expectations. Leverage their knowledge of your nonprofit and their professional expertise. They can tell you how to come into compliance in an efficient and cost-effective manner. Certified public accountants (CPAs) can help companies use SOX compliance as a stepping stone to improved decision making, more efficient processes, and greater confidence in financial reporting.[4]

- *Position your nonprofit to increase its donor base, expand its collaborative relationships, and expand any for-profit components of the nonprofit operations.* Let the world know that you are in compliance! Demonstrating that your nonprofit is in compliance with SOX will position it to increase its revenue by being an attractive vendor or subcontractor to larger nonprofits or businesses. SOX compliance can also help to retain current donors by bolstering confidence in your nonprofit's integrity and transparency. SOX compliance is also a way of presenting business "credentials" that are essential in securing contracts with public-sector (governmental) entities.

FIVE REASONS WHY SOX COMPLIANCE AND BEST PRACTICES WILL ACCELERATE YOUR NONPROFIT'S STRATEGIC PLANNING

1. *The implementation of SOX requirements and best practices will help your nonprofit understand how the organization actually operates.* Tables of

organization attempt to show how the nonprofit ought to work, but instituting SOX requirements and best practices will show how the nonprofit really works. Knowing how the organization actually operates is essential in strategic planning because, in order to introduce change, the planners need to know where to begin.

2. *The implementation of SOX requirements and best practices will facilitate your getting your nonprofit house in order.* Effective strategic planning starts with having an organization that is systematic in its handling of internal operations, its management of documents, and its support of investigating reports of waste, fraud, and abuse.

3. *The process of implementing SOX requirements and best practices will also identify those areas within your nonprofit that need modification and/or need new or different resources to render them functional again.* One of the best by-products of SOX compliance is its ability to identify processes and systems within the nonprofit that need some work. If these areas are fairly extensive, that's fine. At least your nonprofit has an idea of what needs attention. The strategic plan can incorporate those areas of SOX compliance that need additional attention as strategic goals. This will ensure that the problem areas receive the attention and resources that they need.

4. *Introduces a higher level of accountability and transparency by hands-on methods and the integration of SOX best practices into everyday operations.* As the nonprofit continues to implement SOX best practices, the quality of operations will improve because of the increased accountability and transparency. These best practices will accelerate the strategic planning process because a momentum has been established in terms of change and reform.

5. *Once SOX compliance and best practices have been implemented, everyone in your nonprofit should understand where the nonprofit is now, where it wants to go, and what it will need to move to the next level.* Strategic planning begins with an in-depth review of the organizational profile. SOX implementation will provide strategic planners with the depth of information that they need to identify the nonprofit's direction and strategic goals.

NEXT STEPS

Chapter 4 presents efficient ways in which SOX requirements and best practices can be implemented in your nonprofit. Every nonprofit is different, so be sure to read Chapter 4 with your organization in mind. The methods are generic and are easily adjusted to meet the needs of your specific organization.

NOTES

1. Eichenwald, Kurt. 2002. "Arthur Andersen Convicted of Obstruction of Justice." *New York Times*, June 15.
2. BoardSource and Independent Sector. 2003. "The Sarbanes-Oxley Act and Implications for Nonprofit Organizations," retrieved on March 14, 2004, from http://www.boardsource.org/clientfiles/Sarbanes-Oxley.pdf
3. Jackson, Peggy M. 2006. *Sarbanes-Oxley for Small Businesses*. Hoboken, N.J.: John Wiley & Sons.
4. Harrington, Cynthia. 2005. "The Value Proposition." *Journal of Accountancy,* September.

Making SOX Requirements and Best Practices Work for your Nonprofit

Introduction

Chapter 3 described the two provisions of the Sarbanes-Oxley law that are required for all organizations, and the best practices that have emerged from the implementation of the law in the private sector. Implementing the SOX requirements and best practices creates an efficiency of scale in terms of small efforts rendering significant benefits and in understanding how the nonprofit's systems operate independently and at the same time are dependent on other systems.

This chapter will present a streamlined approach to tailoring SOX requirements and best practices to best suit your organization. As you read this chapter and examine the sample documents in the appendices, it's important that you think about how these requirements and best practices would need to be adapted to work in your nonprofit (see Exhibit 4.1). Compliance with new practices and procedures cannot be achieved if the new ways of doing things don't make sense. Keeping things simple and logical helps prevent complex rules and bureaucratic procedures. The level of compliance with any new behaviors is directly correlated with how well the new behaviors are understood. If the rationale is clear, compliance will

EXHIBIT 4.1   SARBANES-OXLEY REQUIREMENTS AND BEST
PRACTICES CHECKLIST

- Does your nonprofit have a whistle-blower protection policy?
- Do your staff and volunteers know how to make a confidential report of waste, fraud, or abuse? Do they know their rights under the whistle-blower protection policy?
- Does your nonprofit have a method for storing and archiving all documents—paper, electronic, and e-mails?
- Does your nonprofit have a policy that prohibits the destruction of documents during an inquiry?
- How are board members recruited and screened for membership on the board?
- Does your nonprofit's senior management recruit board members?
- Are new and current board members required to attend orientation sessions that address their obligations and performance expectations?
- Does your nonprofit allow members of the same family to serve together on the board?
- Does your board meet at regular intervals? Is there an attendance requirement?
- Are minutes kept for all board and committee meetings? How are these minutes stored?
- Does your nonprofit have an audit committee whose role is to oversee the annual audit or financial review (for small nonprofits) and to upgrade the financial literacy of the board?
- Has your nonprofit taken steps to achieve a level of enhanced detail and accuracy in the preparation of IRS Form 990?
- Does your nonprofit have a conflict-of-interest policy and a code of ethics that facilitate greater focus on decision making for the good of the nonprofit?
- Has your nonprofit reviewed and critiqued its internal controls, particularly as these relate to financial operations and compliance with all laws and regulations at the federal, state, and local levels?

probably be pretty good. If the new behaviors don't make sense, they will probably be ignored—or worse yet—sabotaged.

The Two SOX Requirements

Whistle-Blower Protection

The first obligation from SOX that applies to all organizations is the requirement for a documented whistle-blower protection policy. SOX requires all organizations, including nonprofits, to establish a means to collect, retain, and resolve claims regarding accounting, internal accounting controls, and auditing matters (see Exhibit 4.2). The system must allow for such concerns to be submitted anonymously. SOX provides significant protections to whistle-blowers and severe penalties to those that retaliate against them.

EXHIBIT 4.2   **WHISTLE-BLOWER PROTECTION POLICY WORKSHEET**

The Board's Role

- The board needs to review the nonprofit's current whistle-blower protection policy and/or direct the executive director to draft this policy immediately. The SOX requirement is in effect right now. If your nonprofit does not have a whistle-blower protection policy and an employee claims wrongful termination based on whistle-blower activities, your nonprofit could not only lose in subsequent litigation, the failure to have such a policy might also be grounds for punitive damages (which are **not** covered by your insurance) or other sanctions.
- The board needs to ensure that there is a mechanism for staff or volunteers to report retaliatory behavior if they have made a report regarding waste, fraud, or abuse. Putting this in place sends a message to both senior management and staff/volunteers that the board is serious about remaining in compliance with this provision of SOX.

Your nonprofit needs to have:

- A whistle-blower protection policy
- A method for reporting waste, fraud, or abuse
- Procedures for conducting investigations
- Protocols for disseminating findings (in conjunction with your legal counsel)

Whistle-Blower Protection Policy

- The whistle-blower protection policy is being implemented at [your nonprofit] to comply with the Public Company Accounting Reform and Investor Protection Act of 2002 (Sarbanes-Oxley).
- At [your nonprofit], any staff member or volunteer who reports waste, fraud, or abuse will not be fired or otherwise retaliated against for making the report.
- The report will be investigated and even if determined not to be waste, fraud, or abuse, the individual making the report will not be retaliated against. There will be no punishment for reporting problems—including firing, demotion, suspension, harassment, failure to consider the employee for promotion, or any other kind of discrimination.

Methods for Reporting Waste, Fraud, or Abuse

There are several ways in which your staff and volunteers can report suspected waste, fraud, or abuse:

- Contact the nonprofit's ombudsman.
- Call the designated hotline that your nonprofit has set up for this purpose.
- Send an e-mail to a designated address that your nonprofit has established for these types of reports.
- Make the report in writing.

(continued)

EXHIBIT 4.2 (CONTINUED)

Investigating the Report

Your nonprofit would list the steps it would take to:

• Investigate the allegation.
• Disseminate the report on its findings, including providing the person filing a report with a summary of the findings.
• Take steps to deal with the issue addressed, including making operational or personnel changes.
• If warranted, contact law enforcement to deal with any criminal activities.

Your nonprofit's whistle-blower protection needs to include these features:

• *There is a confidential avenue for reporting suspected waste, fraud, and abuse.* Staff and volunteers are not going to report waste, fraud, or abuse if they think they will need to "go public." It is essential that the reporting mechanism you utilize is seen as safe.

• *There is a process to thoroughly investigate any reports.* Equally important is to investigate the report thoroughly to ensure that the situation reported actually is one of waste, fraud, or abuse.

• *There is a process for disseminating the findings from the investigation.* The findings need to be disseminated on a *need-to-know basis.*

• *The employee filing the complaint will not be subjected to termination, firing, or harassment, or miss out on promotion.* This assurance is one of the most important aspects of a whistle-blower protection policy. People do not report incidents of waste, fraud, and abuse because they believe, often accurately, that the whistle-blower will be the one to pay the ultimate price rather than the perpetrator. As noted in Chapter 2, whistle-blowers at Enron were routinely fired.

• *Even if the findings do not support the nature of the complaint, the employee or volunteer who made the complaint will not face any repercussions.* Sometimes people make reports in good faith, but the reality of the situation is quite different. The person making the report should receive an explanation to the extent that the information provided is necessary and sufficient. Confidential information should never be divulged to individuals just because the person mistakenly thought he or she was observing waste, fraud, or abuse. However, whatever it was that prompted the report should be examined and perhaps modified because it gave an incorrect impression.

- *All employees and volunteers should have a copy of the whistle-blower policy and it should be posted in clear view.* This policy should also be covered in any orientation or training programs the organization offers for its employees and volunteers. Orientation and training events provide an opportunity to explain what the whistle-blower protection policy is, how to make a report, how the report is processed, and what the person making the report should expect. These events are also an opportunity to explain to staff and volunteers that reports of waste, fraud, or abuse can be crucial in ensuring the well-being of the nonprofit.

FRAUD: THE PRIMARY REASON FOR WHISTLE-BLOWER PROTECTION

Most of the reasons for whistle-blowing relate to fraudulent activities. Some of the more troublesome areas related to fraud include:

- *Loans, gifts, bonuses, and perks to board members and executives.* Nonprofits often agree to loans and gifts to board members and executives either because the individual is in a financial emergency or as a reward for excellent performance. Nonprofits, particularly in terms of board governance, are under much more scrutiny in terms of the way in which executive compensation packages are approved. The California Nonprofit Integrity Act requires documentation of board approval of executive compensation packages.

- *Expense accounts and travel claims.* Financial misappropriation often is hidden in transactions involving expense accounts and travel claims.

- *Lack of an enforceable conflict-of-interest policy.* Similarly, a conflict-of-interest policy should apply to everyone in the nonprofit.

- *Minimal internal controls.* The nonprofit does not have policies and procedures in place to establish controls on revenue and expenses.

- *The nonprofit's information technology (IT) system needs upgrading.* The nonprofit's databases and other software are not integrated or subject to adequate security measures. This scenario creates additional opportunities to manipulate data and records.

At the very minimum, the above issues should be addressed in the nonprofit's finance policies and human resource policies. The nonprofit's board and executive team lead the way in changing the nonprofit's culture by adopting ethical practices and ensuring that the leadership sets the example by its decisions and actions. Do not expect the rest of the nonprofit's staff and volunteers to change their behavior unless they see that you have adopted these measures as part of daily operations.

Your discussion about fraud needs to be structured in a way that clearly explains to staff and volunteers what waste, fraud, and abuse looks like and how to report these occurrences. The nonprofit needs to establish a mechanism not only to protect whistle-blowers, but to encourage reporting of waste, fraud, or abuse. The sooner that management and senior management know about a potential problem, the sooner the problem can be handled. Consider whistle-blower protection an important factor in your nonprofit's commitment to total quality management. Individuals who report problems with internal controls or procedures should be rewarded! They just saved your nonprofit time, money, and labor. The report might also have identified a problem that, if ignored, over time could have resulted in a crisis.

As the executive director, you need to be open, honest, and frank about how important it is for staff and volunteers to report waste, fraud, and abuse, and how much you value these reports. Your nonprofit might want to offer some incentive for helping the organization save money. The incentive should probably be something that would appeal to the individual, so keep an open mind about what the reward should be. For example, offering hockey tickets to a ballet enthusiast probably won't be well received.

Why Individuals Are Reluctant to Blow the Whistle on Waste, Fraud, and Abuse

Despite federal law prohibiting retaliation, whistle-blowing is often viewed as a career-limiting gesture. Whistle-blowers often discover, despite the considerable financial irregularities they have identified, that they have virtually no support from management. The situation is not remedied and wrongdoers are not held accountable. Negative responses to whistle-blowers can be subtle, such as ostracism or moving the person's office to a less desirable location, but just as effective as explicit retaliation in silencing or discrediting the whistle-blower.

Whistle-blowers are not universally embraced by management in any organization. Often, they are described as "not team players" or are categorized as troublemakers. Management can use tactics such as rumor and innuendo to make the whistle-blower look bad. Other tactics include the silent treatment by supervisors or colleagues or even changing the location of the person's office or the type of equipment that is assigned to them. Management's displeasure is intended to be obvious to the whistle-blower and to everyone else.[1]

The nonprofit's board needs to send a clear message to management, staff, and volunteers that any negative response to a report of waste, fraud, or abuse is unacceptable. Retaliation, no matter how subtle, is *against the law.* Whether management approves of the whistle-blower's message is irrelevant. The whistle-blower protection requirement of SOX is clear about the prohibition against retribution of any kind—even the subtle acts. In today's legal environment, management *can be held responsible* for "punishing" a whistle-blower, even in subtle ways. Having an effective whistle-blower protection policy is important not only because of the SOX legal requirements, but to provide a mechanism to protect the nonprofit's integrity and future viability.

Factors that Support Fraud

Fraud and fraudulent activities don't simply happen overnight. There are supporting factors within a nonprofit that facilitate opportunities for fraud:

- *Incentive.* Individuals who engage in fraudulent activities want to steal and either don't believe they will be caught or believe that there will be few if any consequences for their behavior.

- *The occasion for the fraud to take place.* In other words, there are weak or nonexistent internal controls that provide the opportunity to engage in fraudulent activities. Other occasions can include access to petty cash or other assets that are quickly converted to cash.

- *Sloppy or nonexistent internal controls.* It's easier to cover one's tracks when there are no protocols or records kept.

- *Access to electronic databases and online checking.* Often, electronic records will need to be altered to cover the fraud. Individuals who have access to sensitive databases are in a position to set up sham accounts and issue checks to themselves.

- *The nonprofit's culture, which either denies the possibility of anyone's committing fraud or, even more insidious, transforms staff and volunteers into martyrs.* How many times have you heard people say, "We work so hard here for so little money"?

- *A board and executive team that are asleep at the wheel.* How often do we hear stories about fraud committed at a nonprofit only to learn that the executive director and board knew nothing about it and suspected nothing. That's one of the most important reasons why the board and executive director need to lead the way in talking about fraud and in instituting and enforcing antifraud measures.[2]

SOX requirements will provide individuals with the opportunity to report waste, fraud, or abuse without fear of retaliation. An additional benefit of your nonprofit's document preservation policy is that it will also facilitate more efficient record keeping and provide auditors (external and internal) with better data for their review. The overall strengthening of the internal controls that comes with the implementation of best practices will further reduce the opportunities for fraud and will introduce a change in the nonprofit culture.

Talking to Your Staff and Volunteers about Fraud

Studies have shown that many of the cases involving fraud first involved the chief executive officer (CEO) and/or the chief financial officer (CFO).[3] The fraud began in these corporations, literally, at the top. Recent scandals in the nonprofit world further illustrate that fraudulent behavior is not the exclusive realm of the private sector.

When talking to your staff and volunteers about fraud, it's important to begin with a clear description about what you, the executive director or chair of the board, are *personally* doing to combat fraud. Your nonprofit's board and senior executives will need to adopt a conflict-of-interest policy and a code of ethics (which will be discussed later in the chapter) that includes prohibitions against loans and gifts to management, stringent procedures for travel claims, and management of expense accounts and transparency in their dealings.

Above all, stress that SOX compliance is not a fad and is definitely not going away at your nonprofit! Despite everything you say, what you *do* will be the most effective method of communicating that SOX compliance and ethical behavior is here to stay.

Talking Points in the Discussion about Fraud   The nonprofit executive director needs to lead the way in talking about fraud and needs to be the visible source of policy making in this area. When he or she talks about fraud, the discussion needs to be candid about the factors that support fraud, and why the implementation of SOX requirements and best practices will help the nonprofit reduce the potential for fraud within its operations. It is equally important to emphasize that the board and executive director are committed to whistle-blower protection, and any type of retaliation is to be reported directly to a designated board member.

Don't be sidetracked by the long-time manager, volunteer, or employee whose "feelings will be hurt" if protocols and expectations are changed. The well-being of your nonprofit comes first. These individuals will just have to get over their "hurt" if they want to remain on the staff and volunteers of the nonprofit.

An alternative approach that is generally very effective is to have one of your professional advisers, such as your banker or insurance broker, talk to staff and volunteers about fraud. The perspective of an outside third party is crucial in driving the point home. A financial professional will gladly send the message that you mean business and that fraudulent activities inflict tremendous damage on any nonprofit. Your financial professional can offer suggestions to your staff and volunteers about basic fraud protection and how they play a role in deterring fraud. Communication is key in ensuring that all staff and volunteers understand why reporting waste, fraud, and abuse is expected; what their rights are; and how investigations are conducted and findings presented. Appendix 1 presents a worksheet on the creation of a whistle-blower protection policy.

Document Management and Preservation Policy

Board and Management Team   Because your nonprofit's document management program is required for SOX compliance, the board and senior management need to announce its inception and emphasize that this is not a fad—compliance with this policy is a condition of continued employment. Delegation of responsibilities and accountability is essential in the design of any document management program, but constant communication throughout the organization is also essential. The reason people believe management innovations are fads is that they are not constantly reminded of the change, nor is there sufficient training or personalization of the change. In other words, staff and volunteers do not understand that they have an individual responsibility for compliance, and that the quality of their compliance will be assessed at their next performance evaluation. Enforcement of document management compliance needs to be consistent and a condition of employment. Consequences for failing to comply need to be swift and well publicized.

Policies on document preservation should be developed by the board and senior management. The system you design for document storage, archives, and retrieval must be logical and user friendly. If staff can't understand what it's about, what's expected of them, and why they are being asked to do this, then the probability of success is low. Appendix 2 is a worksheet that you can use to implement a document preservation policy at your nonprofit.

The important talking points of this policy are:

- What the document retention policy is and why it is required by law. It is important that the staff and volunteers understand that document preservation is a component of SOX that applies to all organizations.
- What are the new procedures that emerge from the policy? What are the deliverables that the nonprofit should expect and enforce?
- What does this legal requirement mean for your nonprofit?
- What are the obligations of individual employees to ensure that your nonprofit is in compliance?
- What is expected in terms of new behaviors and procedures and what are the consequences (for individual employees and volunteers) for failing to adhere to the new procedures? Middle and senior management must be prepared to carry out the consequences swiftly to send a strong message throughout the organization.

Like the whistle-blower protection policy, the document preservation policy is an important means by which your nonprofit can grow and thrive. Nonprofits whose document management is chaotic often find themselves facing other, more disastrous, circumstances such as problems preparing Form 990 or responding to an Internal Revenue Service (IRS) inquiry. Instituting and maintaining an effective document management plan that also contains a prohibition against the destruction of documents during an investigation or legal action is one of the most important ways you can help your nonprofit grow and succeed.

Having a solid document management program in place adds value to nonprofits in the form of:

- *Ability to manage institutional knowledge.* Managers, staff, and volunteers know *where* specific documents and records are stored. There is a method that facilitates immediate access, in addition to a set of protocols for archiving documents and, at the appointed time, the destruction of documents.

- *Compliance with SOX, assured by means of a policy prohibiting destruction of documents during an investigation or discovery.* Everyone on the staff knows what the policy is and knows that consequences for noncompliance will be vigorously enforced.

- *Opportunities for continuous improvement.* Change and continuous improvement are accepted parts of the technology applications. The document management program needs to grow, expand, and improve with new technology and methods.

- *Implementing a document management program is one of the methods for communicating management's commitment to change within a nonprofit.* Because document management is required under Sarbanes-Oxley, the enforcement of this policy is an important signal that the nonprofit *will* be in compliance.

- *Make compliance part of the staff's performance reviews.* If a staff is not managing his/her documents per SOX requirements, then this is reflected in performance reviews. The staff's future salary adjustments, or even continued employment can be contingent upon the degree of compliance.

- *Auditors expectations and observations.* The nonprofit's auditors will be examining the way in which documents (electronic and otherwise) are managed, and the way in which technology is used to facilitate SOX compliance.

- *Raises performance levels.* The ability to access files instantly saves time and energy for everyone on the staff. Further, it brings about an efficiency of scale that translates into higher levels of productivity.[4]

Having an integrated document management system ensures that important documents are stored in safe, accessible locations and backed up on a daily basis. This system will introduce a higher level of efficiency and accountability. Each division will have individuals who are responsible for document preservation and whose performance review reflects how well they carry out these responsibilities. As nonprofit operations have become increasingly dependent on technology applications and products, the role of IT has emerged as one of the key operational units within any nonprofit. The executive team is tasked with ensuring that SOX compliance and best practices are implemented, but it is the IT division that will execute the assignment.

Streamlined Method for Implementing a Document Preservation Policy

Establishing a document preservation policy need not be a daunting endeavor. Following are six steps that will speed the process:

Step 1. Consider what types of documents your nonprofit would need to store/archive and be able to retrieve. Examples of documents that need to be stored include:

- Contracts with vendors for services including insurance policies and auditor contracts (particularly to demonstrate that the auditing firm is not providing any other services to your nonprofit)
- Contracts with external clients (such as public sector agencies) to provide services to the external clients
- Contracts with your nonprofit's programmatic clients
- Contracts with your nonprofit's management, staff, and volunteers (if applicable)
- Documents that a regulatory agency requires you to retain such as tax returns, business license documents, vehicle registration forms, and professional licensure documents
- Correspondence with regulators about your nonprofit's operations
- Documents containing information that a regulator would need to review

- Documents required by local, state, and federal law and correspondence regarding these documents
- Documents that have historical, legal, or programmatic significance for your nonprofit
- Instant messages or e-mails that contain negotiations for a contract or other legal agreement
- Any document that would provide proof that your nonprofit took action in a business, contractual, or legal matter
- Financial documents, reports, analyses, and forecasts
- Donor records, history, and correspondence
- Human resource records, including volunteer and board files
- Documents that reflect the sale of property, merchandise, or any tangible or intangible assets

How Long Should These Documents Be Retained?   The length of time that certain documents should be retained is contingent upon the nature of the document. Exhibit 4.3[5] shows a list of sample requirements. Be sure to consult with your accounting professional, insurance professional, or legal counsel to ensure that your nonprofit has established an accurate timeline for archiving documents.

Step 2. Inventory the nonprofit's current record system to determine what records are in use, what records are in storage, and what records

EXHIBIT 4.3   SAMPLE MINIMUM STORAGE REQUIREMENTS

Document	Storage
Accounts receivable and payable ledgers	7 years
Articles of incorporation, charter, bylaws, and minutes	Permanently
Bank reconciliation	3 years
Bank statements, electronic fund transfers, and canceled checks	3 years
Contracts, mortgages, notes, and leases (expired)	7 years
Deeds, mortgages, and bills of sale	Permanently
Payroll records	7 years
Contracts still in effect	Permanently
Correspondence—legal	Permanently
Correspondence—vendors	2 years
Tax returns and worksheets	Permanently
Grants (funded)	7 years after closure

Source: National Association of Veterans Research and Education Foundations.

are archived. This step should also include a review of the types of e-mail messages and instant messages that are routinely transmitted along with attachments.

Step 3. Develop retention rules (based on legal requirements and the operational needs of your nonprofit) and ensure that these rules are clearly disseminated to all staff and volunteers. There needs to be a classification system (develop a simple one) that allows for documents to be classified as "confidential," "private," or other designation that precludes them from general access. As part of this step, it is essential that a training program be developed for staff to ensure that they understand what is expected of them, what the procedures are, and what records they are expected to retain.

Step 4. Develop a process for finding and preserving documents that either will be or are part of an investigation or legal action. There must also be a mechanism for announcing that no documents are to be destroyed until an "all clear" notice is given, as well as stiff consequences for failing to adhere to this directive. Exhibit 4.4 is a worksheet to help your nonprofit develop a policy that prohibits the destruction of documents during specific occasions. Before you announce any policy, be sure to have your legal counsel review and approve the wording.

Step 5. Develop rules for managing, storing, preserving, and archiving electronic messages or other electronic data. The rules should address the important issues, including listing the types of documents that are to be

EXHIBIT 4.4	**PROHIBITION AGAINST DESTROYING DOCUMENTS WORKSHEET**

The nonprofit's document preservation policy needs to include a policy that prohibits destruction of documents during a regulatory or legal investigation.

Talking points:

- When are staff and volunteers prohibited from destroying files? When an instruction is sent to everyone to stop document destruction.
- Staff and volunteers are expected to stop destroying documents until such time that they receive an instruction stating that document destruction can resume.
- Staff and volunteers must always receive permission before documents in any of the document preservation categories are destroyed.

retained and how these documents are to be stored. The process need not be complicated, but the rules need to be standardized—there is no room for "doing your own thing." Staff and volunteers need to understand that they are obligated to adhere to the rules or face the consequences. The rules should also include steps to be taken to ensure that the documents cannot be tampered with, such as using PDF (portable document format) files or passwords. It is particularly important to store financial records in such a way as to ensure that they represent a true and honest picture of the nonprofit's financial profile and/or other financial description. Regulators will need to rely on the accuracy of all of your electronic records—no exceptions.

An important component of this step is the design of a technology policy or the revision of your current technology policy. Exhibit 4.5 is a sample technology policy. The nonprofit's technology policy should include these important points:

- *Clearly state that all aspects of the nonprofit's technology belongs to the nonprofit.* There are *no* expectations of personal privacy when using the nonprofit's technology.

- *Identify all of the nonprofit's technology*—hardware and software including laptop computers, desktop computers, handheld devices such as personal digital assistants (PDAs) and Blackberries, cell phones, Internet access, e-mail, and all software programs purchased through the nonprofit. Be aware that when electronic devices such as laptops or PDAs are "recycled" to another staff member, the hard drive of the device may still contain data, documents, or transactions from the previous employee. It is important to institute a procedure to erase the hard drive once all of the documents have been extracted and stored according to your nonprofit's document retention policy.

- *Develop a policy on the storage and transportation of sensitive information out of your nonprofit's facilities.* Published reports describe multiple scenarios of laptops of bank employees being stolen that contained client financial data. The same thing could happen to your nonprofit if you store sensitive information about donors, clients, or staff on laptops that leave your premises.

EXHIBIT 4.5   TECHNOLOGY POLICY CHECKLIST

- All aspects of the nonprofit's technology belongs to the nonprofit. There are *no* expectations of personal privacy when using the nonprofit's technology.
- E-mail and web access belong to the nonprofit.
- Examples of inappropriate e-mail messages:
  - Jokes
  - Harassment
  - Political commentary, particularly hate messages
  - Anything you wouldn't want to read on the front page of your local newspaper or have CNN broadcast.
- The policy covers all of the nonprofit's technology—hardware and software including laptop computers, desktop computers, handheld devices such as PDAs and Blackberries, cell phones, Internet access, e-mail and all software programs purchased through the nonprofit.
- Requires returning of all electronic devices such as laptops or PDAs when leaving the employ or volunteer assignment of the nonprofit.
- Policy on the storage and transportation of sensitive information on laptops that leave your premises.
- Staff and volunteers who are entrusted with the nonprofit's cell phones, laptops, PDAs, or other electronics need to understand that they will be held personally accountable for the safety of the equipment, the safe use of the equipment, and the security of the data that is stored within these electronics.

Does your nonprofit have a privacy policy that relates to donor information? Information about clients, staff, volunteers? If not, you need to institute one immediately and disseminate the policy(ies) to the various constituencies (see Exhibit 4.6). For example, if your nonprofit has a web site, do you list the names of donors? If you list these names, have each of the donors signed a consent document? In today's world of identity theft and Internet hacking, it is particularly important to protect donors, staff, and board members.

State that when employees leave their job at the nonprofit they will be expected to surrender all technology to the human resources (HR) department prior to their departure. Obtain a signed receipt from HR for all of the equipment that was turned over to them.

Maintaining the System   Specific employees within each division of your nonprofit should be assigned the responsibility and the requisite power and resources for document retention within their division. It is essential that these individuals all have the same training and knowledge of organizational

EXHIBIT 4.6   DONOR PRIVACY CHECKLIST

Do your donors know...

- They have the right to "opt out" of future mailings and phone calls?
- How to indicate that they do not want to receive mailings (paper or e-mail) and phone calls?
- That they must give your nonprofit permission to list their name in a brochure, program, or other material?
- That your nonprofit might sell their donor information to another nonprofit or a vendor?
- That they are under no obligation to give your nonprofit any information that it requests?
- That your nonprofit has a donor privacy statement that is available for their review?

Donor Privacy Statement: Talking Points

- Your nonprofit is committed to maintaining donor privacy. To that end, donors to your nonprofit should expect:
  - That their information will be held in the strictest confidence. *If your nonprofit plans to sell donor information, you must disclose this to potential donors.* If you don't want them to know—don't sell their information!
  - That they will be given information regarding "opt out" features. Donors will be able to "opt out" of paper mailings, e-mails, telephone calls, or other types of solicitations.
  - That they can opt to have their names and information not listed in a brochure, program or other material.
  - That they are under no obligation to provide information such as telephone numbers, addresses and names of family members.
  - Your nonprofit will not ask for sensitive information such as social security numbers or driver's license numbers.
  - That information such as credit card numbers are stored and encrypted to ensure security. If any breech of security takes place, your nonprofit should commit to advising donors in a timely fashion.

---

systems and any technology such as scanners, software, and the like, to ensure that documents are selected, preserved, archived, and able to be retrieved in a consistent, standardized manner.

Establish rules for appropriate and secure electronic transmission of sensitive materials. Work with IT and legal professionals to ensure that these rules are comprehensive and appropriate to your nonprofit.

Step 6. Develop a means by which the document retention system will be audited on a regular basis to ensure that all staff are in compliance with the provisions. Board and staff should understand that the audits will be random and unannounced. Consequences for noncompliance should be meted out quickly to send a message to the entire organization. Please understand that your nonprofit is a business and you need to conduct operations in a business-like fashion. You have an obligation to your donors, your clients, your board, and your staff to ensure that your organization is in compliance with this component of SOX legislation. It's not just a best practice, it is the law and it applies to all organizations in this country, including your nonprofit.[6]

SOX Best Practices

The private sector's experience in implementing SOX requirements has rendered many best practices that are beneficial to nonprofits. SOX best practices are designed to enhance the completeness and reliability of all aspects of your nonprofit's operations.

As discussed in Chapter 3, these best practices include:

- *Internal controls.* Each department within the nonprofit must have a system of internal controls, particularly as these relate to financial operations and compliance with all laws and regulations at the federal, state, and local level that reduces the potential for waste, fraud, and abuse, but also ensures that the nonprofit's property, valuables, and other assets are protected.

- *Adherence to policies and procedures and enforcement.* Once new policies and procedures are in place for SOX compliance, it is important to maintain these practices. It's just human nature to let new standards lapse. For this reason it is essential to ensure that reverting to the old ways is met with unpleasant consequences.

- *Transparency at all levels of management,* including the board, and in all transactions, including travel claims and reimbursements. The board needs to insist that there are written procedures for filing travel and reimbursement claims and that these procedures are enforced—even by means of unannounced audits.

- *Conflict-of-interest policy* that facilitates greater focus on decision making for the good of the nonprofit.

- *Code of ethics* for board and senior management that precludes any loans to directors, officers, management, or staff of the nonprofit.

- *Enhanced detail and accuracy in the preparation of IRS tax documents* in the annual submission of IRS 990 filings. Failure to submit a 990 is no longer an option.

- *Appointing an audit committee* whose role is to oversee the annual audit or financial review (for small nonprofits) and to upgrade the financial literacy of the board. The audit committee is the link between the board and its auditor or financial reviewer. The audit committee is an important element in ensuring that the board understands the results of the annual audit or financial review (for small nonprofits) and that the board's skills in reading and interpreting financial statements is kept up to date. The intent of this best practice is the complete independence of the auditor and the audit committee.

- *Segregation of auditor's duties.* If your nonprofit has an auditor that not only audits the nonprofit's books, but also does the nonprofit's IRS 990 filings or other tasks, the nonprofit should either retain a new auditor or retain an accounting professional to complete the other tasks. This means that if the person who is currently conducting the nonprofit's audit or financial review also prepares the nonprofit's IRS 990 form, then the individual must divest him/herself from one of these roles. The intent of SOX legislation is to segregate these duties. An auditor or auditing firm that provides services to a nonprofit in addition to conducting an audit presents a conflict of interest. The spirit of this SOX best practice also emphasizes the need to ensure the ongoing independence of the auditor by changing auditors every three to five years. If the nonprofit is working with a large auditing firm, then the firm needs to rotate the auditors assigned to the nonprofit. This best practice has generated some resistance by smaller auditing firms, but nonetheless independence does not exist iteratively—the auditor is either fully independent or not!

- *Certified financial statements.* The nonprofit's board and senior management is ultimately accountable for the accuracy and integrity of the nonprofit's financial statements as well as the nonprofit's IRS 990 forms. The board needs to ensure that the nonprofit's executive director, CEO, or CFO can validate the accuracy of the nonprofit's financial statements.

"For a nonprofit organization, CEO and CFO sign-off on financial statements would not carry the weight of law [unless it is required under state law], but it would signal the importance that the CEO, in particular, pays to understanding the nonprofit's financial condition. . . . Signing off on the financial statements provides formal assurance that both the CEO and CFO have reviewed them carefully and stand by them" (www.guidestar.org).

- *Improved governance* and a nonprofit board that understands its role as ultimately accountable for the actions of the nonprofit and is willing to take steps to enhance professional development for each member.[7]

MAKING BEST PRACTICES WORK FOR YOUR NONPROFIT

Internal Controls

All of the nonprofit's departments need to have solid internal controls. The nonprofit's commitment to adopting and maintaining SOX best practices can be demonstrated in a review of internal controls. The process and outcomes can be used to measure the development of the platinum standard. Compliance cannot simply be a rote operation; it must be demonstrated that the commitment to excellence transcends all levels of the organization and is evident in all of the operational systems and in the symbiotic relationship that exists among the various systems within the organization.

Information Technology   One nonprofit was a household name because of its environmental work. Its web site led the viewer through all the various aspects of its work. It even had a link for individuals to make donations. The development director and the technology director were shocked to discover that a porn site was soliciting donations for the nonprofit through a link in the porn site's web page. Viewers of the porn site were also directed—via a link—to the environmental group's site. How did the environmentalists ever find out? The owners of the porn site proudly sent the environmental group a check for the donations that they had collected! The environmentalists' attorney sent the porn site a cease-and-desist letter and returned the check.[8]

Technology plays an important role in compliance and best practices. Implementation of SOX best practices in the area of IT and electronic document management compliance can serve to strengthen internal controls; raise awareness of cyber risks throughout the organization; produce a higher level of efficiency and productivity; and maintain public trust by keeping electronic access to web sites, databases, and confidential information safe.

SOX best practices have some additional benefits for IT as well. Public expectations such as putting the Form 990 on the web site can be achieved without compromising sensitive data on the page with the major donors. The way in which SOX best practices are implemented can serve as the beginning of a sea change within the organization. As we have seen in the passage of California SOX clone legislation, it is only a matter of time before many of these best practices either become law or are codified in the regulatory requirements of federal agencies such as the IRS. As always, the issue of technology can be something of a hot button for employees and volunteers who are either not technology conversant, or are reluctant to model new behavior.

Technology and its application have become the backbone of nonprofit operations. Virtually all nonprofit organizations utilize technology to some degree, whether in the use of computers, databases, Internet access, web sites, PDAs, laptops, notebooks, cell phones, pagers, or voice mail. The proliferation of technology is a double-edged sword. While technology can facilitate higher and more efficient levels of productivity, it is also an integral part of SOX compliance and adaptation of best practices. The bar has been raised permanently in terms of degree of compliance and utilizing technology to strengthen the nonprofit's internal controls. There's no going back!

Applying the lessons learned from the private sector. The private sector is an important source of learning about the adaptation of best practices. Private-sector firms have learned that adaptation of best practices that closely approximate full compliance are considered essential in today's business environment for their financial viability and competitive positioning. Lessons learned include:

- *IT is an essential component in the implementation of SOX document management compliance.* The preservation and proper storage of electronic documents, including e-mail, instant messages, and voice mail, are critical elements in the nonprofit's overall document management compliance plan. Compliance is based on preservation of all vital records and the ability to retrieve important documents when needed.

- *Document management practices must be extended to electronic documents, databases, and software.* Everyone in the nonprofit needs to understand that the policies and procedures in the document preservation policy apply to electronic documents, databases, and software. Electronic documents can be created in an array of electronic devices such as laptops, PDAs, and cell phones (messages and voice mail).

- *Everyone in the organization needs to understand and comply with the technology policy and IT procedural norms.* The nonprofit should have a technology policy, and the IT department needs to have written policies and procedures.

- *Continuous quality assurance.* Continuous quality improvement in the utilization of technology within the nonprofit is crucial to the success of internal controls.

- *Create a checklist for IT role in SOX compliance and best practices in a nonprofit.* The role of IT in the nonprofit has changed dramatically over the last 10 years. Nonprofits, like virtually all other types of organizations, live and die by the quality of their IT functions.

- *Know what types of technology your nonprofit has in terms of hardware, software, PDAs, cell phones, laptops, and voice mail and who has it.* Many nonprofits have no idea what their technology inventory would look like. Often, this is the case because there is no centralized function for ordering electronic equipment, software, and hardware. Tracking the distribution of the nonprofit's technology is essential to determine what electronics the staff or volunteers have in their possession. Even more perplexing is the lack of appropriate systems to ensure that this equipment and software is used appropriately and returned to the organization when the staff member or volunteer using it leaves.

- Develop a policy on the storage and transportation of sensitive information out of your nonprofit's facilities. Published reports describe multiple scenarios of laptops of bank employees being stolen that contained client financial data. The same thing could happen to your nonprofit if you store sensitive information about donors, clients, or staff on laptops that leave your premises.

Your Nonprofit's Web Site Your nonprofit's web site is the electronic "face" of your organization. The way in which it is designed, its features (which make it user friendly—or not) and the content say important things about your organization. Some nonprofits utilize their web sites to collect donations, sell merchandise, or respond to a global disaster. The nonprofit's document preservation policy should also include those "documents" that are pages on the web site such as:

- Your nonprofit's IRS 990 filings
- Documents that demonstrate SOX compliance and best practices—put evidence on your web site
- Reports, information about programs, staff bios, volunteer profiles, and the like

Your nonprofit's web site can also be the portal for cyber attacks, hacking, and even the compromise of sensitive information such as donor credit card numbers if these are used to make donations online. Internal controls for IT need to address the potential for these problems.

Web site security. Security is rapidly becoming one of the most significant challenges to any web site—nonprofit or private sector. Nonprofit web sites need to have firewalls and encryption software to protect donor information and to ensure that transactions online with donors are secure. When donors put their credit card number on your web site, they and you need to feel confident that this sensitive information is properly encrypted and transported to the correct location. You should also consider including recommendations for safety in online transactions such as using a credit card rather than a debit card, checking credit card statements to ensure that all the transactions are accurate, and, if possible, including a link to your local Better Business Bureau, Chamber of Commerce, or nonprofit clearinghouse to verify that you are a member in good standing.

Who owns your web site? This may appear to be a nonsensical question, but consider the case of a small dance company. The company had a volunteer who spent a significant amount of time working on projects. In fact, this volunteer seemed to be everywhere at all times. The volunteer offered to design the dance company's web site, and his efforts were lauded. One board member, however, found this individual's activities, as well as his whole demeanor, suspicious. The board member went to the website www.whois.com and looked up the dance company. Guess who owned the dance company's web site? That's right—the volunteer. Judging from his reaction when confronted, he never thought anyone from the board would ever think to check. The board had to request that the hosting service for the web site take it down until the matter was settled. The dance company had to pay the volunteer before he agreed to surrender the rights to the web site.[9]

Finance   The importance of internal financial controls is so great that many people believe that the financial controls are the internal control system. While this is not true, financial controls are key controls required for an effective internal control system and form the basis of a safe and sound organization. The challenge of designing financial controls is greater for nonprofits, as their financial reporting is not as minutely scrutinized as that of public organizations. While the overall internal control system is important, this section focuses on financial controls.

Financial controls are internal controls designed to protect the nonprofit's assets and ensure accurate financial reporting. These are standards established by the nonprofit to ensure accuracy, timeliness, and completeness of financial data as well as compliance with internal and external policies and regulations. A properly designed and consistently enforced system of financial controls helps management and the board of directors to safeguard and ascertain that assets and financial records are not stolen, misused, or accidentally destroyed. Also, accurate financial reporting provides useful and reliable information for sound decision making. Implementing and maintaining internal financial controls is an important aspect of running a successful nonprofit.

Other than theft, money can disappear due to improper spending controls. For example, if there is no financial control that limits spending or scrutinizes expenses, an employee might choose to travel in business class instead of economy class, resulting in much higher travel expenses for the nonprofit. All nonprofits should welcome internal financial control. A good control system should cover all individual elements of the nonprofit's financial administration.

Streamlined methods for financial internal controls. If your nonprofit has very few internal controls for financial operations, here are some recommended actions that will quickly render benefits:[10]

- *Cash receipts.* Cash receipts relates to issuance of receipts, acceptance of cash, deposits, and recording of cash in any form. It includes currency and checks. Financial control helps to ensure that all cash intended for the organization is received, promptly deposited, properly recorded, reconciled, and kept under adequate security.

- *Cash disbursement.* For an effective financial control of any cash disbursements it is essential to develop policies so that documentation is presented before cash is disbursed, and forms are completed with receipts attached. It is also important to segregate tasks. Different people should be required authorize payments, sign checks, and record payments in books, and reconcile the bank statements. It is important to ensure that the cash disbursement is made under proper authorization and for valid business reasons. All disbursements are recorded properly.

- *Accounts receivable.* Accounts receivables, particularly as this relates to the payments of donor pledges to the nonprofit, are amounts owned to the nonprofits from sales or delivery of services to its clientele made on credit. A good financial control to handle accounts receivable is to properly record the receivable, which is usually classified as a donation. The budget for the nonprofit should also include a percentage for uncollectible pledges.

- *Accounts payable.* Accounts payable are amounts due to vendors, suppliers, or others from whom the nonprofit has received goods or services on credit. A proper financial control of accounts payable ensures that all invoices are legitimate and accurate, they are properly recorded, and payment is made to the right supplier. Do the nonprofit's staff and/or volunteers have access to credit cards or vendor accounts? If so, the specific product or service purchased needs to be recorded and the accounts need to be reconciled at least on a monthly basis. When a staff member leaves the employ of the nonprofit, any credit cards must be turned in and vendors notified that the staff member is no longer employed by the nonprofit.

- *Petty cash.* Petty cash is a cash fund maintained for payment of small incidental purchases or reimbursements. Dealing in cash represents an extra degree of risk, so a greater degree of care needs to be exercised. Proper controls of petty cash could include the following rules:

- Petty cash should always be kept under lock and key.
- There should be tab on the minimum and the maximum amount to be kept in the fund.
- There is a limit on the amount of petty cash that can be used for a single disbursement.
- The fund should be enough to cover petty cash expenditures for a month.
- There must be a process for petty cash disbursement that includes documentation such as receipts or other forms signed by a manager.

- *Segregation of duties.* Financial control includes written policies that ensure the segregation of responsibilities. The segregation of financial management responsibilities means that the same person may **not** conduct all of the steps in processing check requests or other financial activities. The segregation of responsibilities reduces a person's opportunity to commit and conceal fraud or errors. It also includes rotation of duties. Duties should be divided between staff to reduce the opportunity for errors and frauds. For example, in the case of paying invoices, one person should authorize the payment, another should draw the checks and record the payment in proper books of accounts, a third person should sign the checks, and fifth person should reconcile the bank statements. Since each individual is given the ownership of that particular task, any break in the flow immediately flags the person who committed the fraud.

- *Check signing.* A simple control regarding check signing requires checks to be signed by at least two different people if the amounts of purchases go above a certain level. The purpose of this is to create a check and balance on check signing and give the decisions of whom to pay, how much to pay, why to pay, and when to pay to multiple individuals. This makes misappropriation of funds difficult.

- *Documentation for all payments.* Every payment should be supported by the original invoice, with receipts and other documentation attached to the invoice. When the payment is made by check, the entry should be recorded; the name of the person or firm to whom payment is made should be recorded, and the check number, check date, and check amount should also be noted. The names of the check-signing authorities should also be recorded and their signatures obtained.

- *Employee advances.* Employee advances should be for business-related expenses *only.* There should *never* be salary advances, loans, or any other disbursement of cash beyond salaries to *anyone—not board members, not managers, not volunteers—no one!*

If there is a cash advance for a legitimate business expense, there should be guidelines defining the maximum cash advance that can be given to an employee, documentation of the cash advance request, and approval of the request before the cash advance is made. The loop does not close until final documentation regarding the use of the cash is received and verified. For example, an employee might receive a cash advance to purchase an office printer based on a quote. The transaction closes only after submission of final original receipts from the vendor to make sure there are no differences in the quote and final invoice as well as safeguard that the employee does not return the purchase using the original receipt and exchange the item for something less costly.

- *Employee travel.* Employee travel expense claims must be subject to clear *written* guidelines as to what expenses are and are not allowed (see Exhibit 4.7). Copies of these guidelines must be distributed to anyone who is about to travel on behalf of the nonprofit. Travel on behalf of the nonprofit should be approved in writing and in advance of a trip. Receipts must accompany every expense—no exceptions. Control guidelines for employee travel include specified modes of travel, travel notice, travel approvals from employees' managers, and documented justification of the need to travel. If the employee makes the travel arrangements, the employee must provide proper documentation in terms of original receipts and a manager-approved form for reimbursement.

- *Bank statement reconciliation.* Every month your nonprofit will receive at least one bank statement. When the bank statement comes in it should be automatically forwarded to the executive director, CFO, or other manager who does not handle direct financial processing on a day-to-day basis.

    Bank statement reconciliation is the process of systematically comparing the cash balance as reported by the bank with the cash balance on the company's books and explaining any differences

EXHIBIT 4.7   TRAVEL CLAIMS POLICY CHECKLIST

- Travel claims are submitted on a specific form designed by the nonprofit. The form needs to capture the name of the staff/volunteer/board member, dates traveled, purpose of travel, listing of expenses, and documentation attached (original documentation should be required).
- The travel claim indicates the purpose of the trip, who authorized the travel, and a copy of the documentation.
- If the travel claim includes reimbursement for meals, the purpose of the meal and the names of the guests is included. For example, if the meal was a business lunch as part of attending a conference, the receipt for the meal needs to be included and any guests or clients should be listed.
- If parking or transportation to the airport is an authorized expenditure, the travel claim also needs to have either a receipt for parking or a mileage listing.
- The nonprofit should specify the time frame that a travel claim needs to be filed, for example, within 10 business days of returning to the office.
- The travel expense policy includes a list of authorized expenditures. Any expenditures that are not included as authorized expenditures on the list must be approved by the CFO or treasurer before they can be reimbursed.
- Travel claims will not be paid unless the form is completed correctly and there is supporting documentation for all expenses.
- The executive team and/or the board's executive committee will make random and unannounced examinations of travel claims within a specific time frame to ensure compliance.

between them. The executive director or CFO needs at least to look over the bank statement and assign the reconciliation process to a person who is not the bookkeeper or accountant. Reconciliation makes sure that the balance of the bank statement, checkbook balance, and the balance in the accounting book (i.e., the ledger and the journal), all tally/agree with each other.

In today's era of online banking, there are now services that the bank can provide that will reduce the potential for fraudulent activity. However, sometimes the bank statement and the checkbook do not match. Some of the reasons why discrepancies may occur include:

- Checks may be issued by the nonprofit in one month but might not be processed by the payee in the same month.
- Interest may be credited or debited to the nonprofit's bank account but it might not be recorded in the nonprofit's books.

- The amount of the check may have been altered by the payee.
- Transfers might be recorded in the books of accounts in a particular month but not recorded in the same month in the bank account.
- Checks could have been stolen from the nonprofit and forged.
- There may be some arithmetic mistakes or other recording errors made by the nonprofit or by the bank.

Whatever the reason for differences between the amounts in the nonprofit's books and the bank statement, reconciliation of the statement should find it and prompts any necessary corrective action.

Human Resource Management

When a nonprofit hires an individual as an employee or permits an individual to volunteer, the organization requires that the individual provide certain types of personal information. Employees are generally required to provide sensitive information such as their Social Security number, names, and contact information for next of kin or other family members, and possibly document numbers that reflect a particular immigration status.

Privacy issues have become more complex because of the proliferation of cell phones, PDAs, laptops, and other electronics. Additionally, Internet access, and e-mail have also contributed to privacy infringement. Although privacy concerns apply to other areas within the nonprofit such as client services and fundraising, the human resources division is responsible for maintaining the privacy and security of personnel records of staff and volunteers.

Privacy Issues and Access to HR Records   Human Resources document preservation guidelines need to ensure that steps are taken to protect confidential records and sensitive information. Because today's personnel records are most likely kept on databases, it is important to work collaboratively with the nonprofit's IT division to ensure that access to sensitive information is restricted. Individuals who have access to these records should be carefully screened, including background and credit checks, and should also be closely supervised.

Identity Theft   In today's world of identity theft, databases, and electronic files can be fertile sources of information for thieves. The problem is that the identity thieves can be located in the same workplace as the victims. How easy does your nonprofit make it for identity theft?

Personnel files should be treated as highly confidential, particularly if these files are stored electronically. All databases should be password protected, and protocols should be in place to ensure that staff do not leave their workstations with a confidential file on the screen. Similarly, if personnel files are in paper files, these files should never be permitted to be left unattended on a desk or in an unlocked file cabinet. Salary spreadsheets, benefits documents, and the like need to be similarly secured.

Trash cans and recycle bins are gold mines to identity thieves. The HR department should invest in several sturdy shredders. All paper that is disposed from this department should first be shredded. The trash can is for waste other than paper.

Knowledge is power! Talk to staff and volunteers about how to protect themselves from identity theft and how to routinely check their credit card invoices and credit reports for evidence of improper charges or the creation of new accounts. The more that staff and volunteers are informed, the better they will understand and comply with the precautions your nonprofit has implemented.

Adherence to Policies and Procedures and Enforcement

Once new policies and procedures are in place for SOX compliance, it is important to maintain these practices. It's just human nature to let new standards lapse. For this reason it is essential to ensure that reverting to the old ways is met with unpleasant consequences.

Transparency at All Levels of Management

In today's legal and legislative environment all organizations including nonprofits are expected to be demonstrating transparency at all levels of management including the board. Transparency and accountability need to be built in to all policies and procedures and in all transactions including travel claims and reimbursements. Transparency begins at the top. The board needs to insist that there are written procedures for filing travel and reimbursement claims and that these procedures are enforced—even by means of unannounced audit.

Conflict-of-Interest Policy

Contrary to what many nonprofit executives and board members believe, disclosing that you may have a potential conflict of interest is not a crime against humanity! A conflict of interest is simply that—a situation that presents a real or possible conflict of interest for the executive director, manager, or board member. The individual executive or board member is not "guilty" of anything by disclosing that he or she has a potential conflict of interest. Actually, this type of disclosure is something to be applauded! The important next step is to have the potential conflict of interest documented via a conflict-of-interest statement that all board members—and senior staff—should submit on an annual basis or in the event that the board member learns of a potential conflict of interest. A sample conflict-of-interest policy and letter is in Appendix 4.

Once the conflict of interest is documented, then the individual should be excused from the conversation/vote whenever their participation would be inappropriate. The minutes should reflect that Ms./Mr. X was excused from the discussion on the nonprofit's insurance coverage because s/he is a member of the insurance company's board. It is important to ensure that a conflict of interest is clearly addressed and documented so that the board can focus on making good business decisions.[11]

Code of Ethics

The nonprofit should have a code of ethics for board and senior management that precludes any loans to directors, officers, management, or staff of the nonprofit. The board needs to adopt a policy strictly prohibiting personal loans to any director or officer and an HR policy that prohibits lending money to the CEO, executive director, CFO, or other staff. This policy describes the types of behavioral expectations that relate to the roles of board member and member of senior management. One provision that is particularly significant is the prohibition against any type of loan or financial gift by the nonprofit to a board member or member of the staff at any level. No exceptions should *ever* be made to these policies. A sample code of ethics is in Appendix 5.

Enhanced Detail and Accuracy in the Preparation of IRS Tax Documents

The testimony of the IRS commissioner in the 2004 and 2005 Senate Finance Committee hearings was very clear in the assertion that the IRS has received additional funding to ensure compliance and accuracy in the annual submission of IRS 990 filings. Failure to submit a 990 is no longer an option.

Appointing an Audit Committee

An audit committee is a committee whose role is to oversee the annual audit or financial review (for small nonprofits) and to upgrade the financial literacy of the board. The audit committee is the link between the board and its auditor or financial reviewer. The audit committee is an important element in ensuring that the board understands the results of the annual audit or financial review (for small nonprofits) and that the board's skills in reading and interpreting financial statements is kept up to date. The intent of this best practice is the complete independence of the auditor and the audit committee. Appendix 3 presents suggested procedures and protocols for an audit committee.

Segregation of Auditor's Duties

If your nonprofit has an auditor that not only audits the nonprofit's books, but also does the nonprofit's IRS 990 filings or other tasks, the nonprofit should either retain a new auditor or retain an accounting professional to complete the other tasks. This means that if the person who is currently conducting the nonprofit's audit or financial review also prepares the nonprofit's IRS 990 form, then the individual must divest him- or herself from one of these roles. The intent of SOX legislation is to segregate these duties. An auditor or auditing firm that provides services to a nonprofit in addition to conducting an audit presents a conflict of interest. The spirit of this SOX best practice also emphasizes the need to ensure the ongoing independence of the auditor by changing auditors every three to five years. If the nonprofit is working with a large auditing firm, then the firm needs to rotate the auditors assigned to the nonprofit. This best practice has generated some "pushback" by smaller auditing firms as evidenced by their e-mail to this author, but nonetheless "independence" does not exist iteratively—the auditor is either fully independent or not!

Certified Financial Statements

The nonprofit's board and senior management is ultimately accountable for the accuracy and integrity of the nonprofit's financial statements as well as the nonprofit's IRS 990 forms. The board needs to ensure that the nonprofit's executive director, CEO, or CFO can validate the accuracy of the nonprofit's financial statements. "For a nonprofit organization, CEO and CFO sign-off on financial statements would not carry the weight of law [unless it is required under state law], but it would signal the importance that the CEO, in particular, pays to understanding the nonprofit's financial condition. . . . Signing off on the financial statements provides formal assurance that both the CEO and CFO have reviewed them carefully and stand by them" (www.guidestar.org).

Improved Governance

One of the most important outcomes from the implementation of SOX requirements and best practices is board development. The nonprofit board must understand its role as ultimately accountable for the actions of the nonprofit and is willing to take steps to enhance professional development for each member.

Next Steps

The implementation of SOX requirements and best practices is the first step in designing a solid and effective strategic plan. Before you begin to implement this list of requirements and best practices, take a look at the policies, procedures, and protocols that you already have in place. You may simply need to document the practices you already have in place or make some simple upgrades. Your nonprofit need not reinvent the wheel if you do have systems in place. The design of your internal controls need not be limited to the functional areas discussed in this chapter. Be sure that your nonprofit has internal controls for every department within your nonprofit.

Mapping out a strategy for SOX implementation is essential to managing your time effectively.

▊ NOTES

1. Sinclair, Matthew. 2004. "Nonprofit Whistleblowers Need Protection." *Nonprofit Times,* June 1.
2. Jackson, Peggy M. 2006. *Sarbanes-Oxley for Small Businesses.* Hoboken, N.J.: John Wiley & Sons.
3. COSO. 1999. *Fraudulent Financial Reporting: 1987–1997: An Analysis of U.S. Public Companies—Executive Summary and Introduction.* Retrieved on April 29, 2005, from http://www.coso.org/publications/ executive_summary_fraudulent_financial_reporting.htm
4. Davis, Linda J. 2005. "Compliance Programs in 2005: What Is Good Enough?" IDC/Kahn Conference, May 12.
5. National Association of Veterans' Research and Education Foundations. 2005. "Impact of the 2002 Sarbanes-Oxley Act (SOX) on Nonprofits." Washington, D.C.
6. Jackson, Peggy M., and Toni E. Fogarty. 2006. *Sarbanes Oxley and Nonprofit Management.* Hoboken, N.J.: John Wiley & Sons, pp. 135–142.
7. Id., pp. 32–33.
8. Id., pp. 129.
9. Id., pp. 142–143.
10. Id., pp. 183–188.
11. Discussion of best practices is adapted from samples in Jackson, Peggy M., and Toni E. Fogarty. 2005. *Sarbanes-Oxley and Nonprofits: A Guide to Gaining Competitive Advantage.* Hoboken, N.J.: John Wiley & Sons.

CHAPTER 5

SOX Best Practices and Your Authentic Organization

Introduction

A mistake is an event, the full benefit of which has not yet been turned to your advantage.[1]

How can a team of committed managers with individual IQs above 120 have a collective IQ of 63?[2]

Peter Senge

The only things that evolve by themselves in an organization are disorder, friction and malperformance....My best book would have been Managing Ignorance, and I'm very sorry I didn't write it.[3]

Peter Drucker

Ignorance isn't what you don't know, it's what you know wrong.

Yogi Berra

Nonprofits often have challenges in introducing the changes that are associated with SOX best practices, establishing internal controls, and creating the type of momentum that would result in effective strategic planning. Organizational dysfunction is often the underlying cause of many operational difficulties in nonprofits. Does your nonprofit have problems with:

- Keeping top-notch employees or volunteers?
- Employees and volunteers who have been with the nonprofit so long that their productivity has waned?
- Maintaining a solid donor base?
- Having proposals funded?
- Public credibility? Do funders, the public sector, donors, and the community ignore or discount the value of your nonprofit?
- Keeping a professional-looking workplace?
- Disorganization of files, reports, and other important business materials?

All of these problems point to dysfunction within your nonprofit's organization. The implementation of SOX requirements and best practices can begin the process of healing your dysfunctional organization, but unless your nonprofit comes to terms with the reasons *why* the organization is dysfunctional, then you will find that there will be significant resistance to SOX as well as strategic planning.

In this chapter, we will discuss:

- Why nonprofits have difficulty *really solving* organizational and operational problems. Why do the same problems keep coming back?
- Why SOX best practices can help the organization to craft a more effective method for identifying the actual sources of problems and craft more effective solutions.
- How the nonprofit's board might be contributing to the overall organizational dysfunction and how SOX compliance can mitigate these problems.
- Why strategic planning is a waste of time unless the nonprofit does something about organizational dysfunction.

Why Do Nonprofits Have Difficulty *Really Solving* Organizational and Operational Problems? Why Do the Same Problems Keep Coming Back?

For many nonprofits, problem solving involves finding the quickest and cheapest bandage to make it go away. This type of superficial response rarely is effective. Why? Nonprofits often do not recognize that serious problems exist until either a crisis erupts or some other disruptive incident occurs that fully grasps their attention. Crises rarely emerge out of nowhere. The nonprofit is responding to what Edgar Schein calls disconfirming data.[4] Disconfirming data is compelling information that describes why the current path of behavior is no longer an option. Clues abound that the current path or options exercised are not working, but nonprofit leaders are often in denial until something happens that can't be ignored.

Problems are often ignored because nonprofit management tends to be more concerned about relationship rather than task. In other words, nonprofit managers are so focused on not hurting feelings or ruffling feathers that they cannot summon the political will to make difficult decisions, including taking the necessary steps to get at the root of the problem. Bandages are quicker, easier, and more politically correct.

To prepare to engage in strategic planning, a nonprofit needs to learn how to *fully* solve problems. A quick fix will make the obvious symptoms go away, but the underlying problem still exists because the decision makers did not take the time to dig deeper to identify the actual source of the problem. For example, if you had a lamp that had a burned-out light bulb, you would probably try to fix the problem by changing out the light bulb. What if the next light bulb burned out, and then the next—what would you do? You would either throw out the lamp or take it to a repair shop to determine what is the underlying cause of the problem. Replacing the light bulb is a bandage approach that probably would work fine except if the lamp had a short circuit. Obviously, organizations are more complex than lamps. Problems that recur need to be subject to more intense investigation to determine the root cause. The difference between a bandage approach and a more in-depth *solution* is the degree to which the nonprofit is committed to identifying *why the problem exists* and to *changing the dynamics that are causing the problem*.

SOX and Problem Solving

SOX requirements and best practices help the organization to design a more effective method for identifying the actual sources of problems and create more effective solutions. At the heart of all of the SOX practices is a method of organizing documents and records to maximize accountability and transparency within the organization. That means that as these practices are put into place, the shadow practices or even outright inappropriate practices will come to light. Nonprofit managers will come face to face with the level of dysfunction that may reside in their organizations.

Anatomy of a Dysfunctional Nonprofit   Dysfunction within a nonprofit can be insidious, or it can be very obvious. Sometimes the most obvious clue that there is dysfunction in a nonprofit is by the fact that nothing ever gets done! There's always an *excuse*, but the bottom line is that the nonprofit has become stagnant in its programs, fund-raising, and purpose within the community.

Some nonprofits mask their dysfunction around an aura of busy-ness. Yet others have highly dysfunctional boards, or management teams, or rank and file. Each of these groups can imprint their particular brand of malignancy on the nonprofit. Sometimes an autocratic leader, perhaps the founder of the organization, is the source—and even a continuing source of dysfunction after he or she is fired. In one such instance, a nonprofit's board terminated the highly dysfunctional founder of the organization but allowed the individual to remain on their board! Why? The board thought this person would be helpful in fund-raising! Such obtuse rationale is not the stuff of fiction—it happens every day.

Dysfunction rapidly infects the systems of the organization until the entire organization suffers from its effects. The implementation of SOX requirements and best practices can have an antidotal effect on organizational dysfunction. Exhibit 5.1 summarizes common symptoms that signal organizational dysfunction and the mitigating effect of SOX implementation.

Organizational Culture

When a new staff member joins your nonprofit, how do they learn what to do and how to do it? Usually, there is some type of formal orientation that

EXHIBIT 5.1   **ORGANIZATIONAL DYSFUNCTION AND SARBANES-OXLEY REMEDIES**

Symptom	Source of Dysfunction	SOX Remedy
Senior management ignores directive of executive director	Chain of command is compromised. Job descriptions and roles not clear. Failure to impose significant consequences for ignoring a superior.	SOX establishes rigorous internal controls that include safeguards against tampering. Chain-of-command internal control can be established with specified consequences for failure to comply.
Financial statements not produced on time or in a professional format	Internal controls lacking. Staff not held accountable for failing to meet deadlines.	Internal controls for financial management are a cornerstone of SOX best practices. Consequences established for failure to meet deadlines.
Staff refuse to comply with directives such as document retention policy	Organizational culture does not support individual accountability. Management does not reinforce accountability with consequences.	Board accountability dictates that controls are put into place that would make the current behavior subject to strict consequences including termination.
Forms 990 are never submitted on time—sometimes more than one year passes before they are submitted	Board lax in holding management accountable for compliance with IRS regulations.	Board accountability and financial internal controls create an environment in which compliance with IRS regulations is essential. Auditors will note noncompliance in management letter.
No policy in place to track credit card expenditures by staff and management	Organizational culture supports naïve belief that staff and management would not misappropriate funds. Lax tracking of financials due to inattention.	Financial internal controls establish a mechanism for rigorous tracking of all charges on nonprofit accounts—credit card and merchant accounts. Consequences for failure to comply could include termination or criminal charges.
Executive compensation packages are never questioned by the board	Board does not understand its governance role. Management may have endeavored to "stack" the board with friends.	Board accountability includes members being held personally responsible for all board decisions, particularly those around executive pay.
Board members sporadically attend board meetings—difficult to obtain a quorum.	Board members do not understand their governance obligations and are not required to comply with these obligations.	Board members are held to a much higher level of accountability in their governance functions.

provides the new staff member with formal information such as the nonprofit's history, financial information, and table of organization. But how does the new staff member learn what's really going on in the workplace? This type of learning often takes place over the person's first weeks and months during lunch, over coffee, or during informal chat at the water cooler.

So what is organizational culture? Organizational culture is a system of shared basic assumptions that helps people within the organization to cope with external forces, solve problems, and pass along the learned methods for dealing with operational issues.[5]

Learning to understand a nonprofit is much like peeling an onion—there are layers upon layers to peel back. Nonprofits aren't just the people that populate them, although the people can be the face of a nonprofit. From deep within nonprofits come the rules—written and unwritten—about how things are done, how problems are solved, and what's valuable. In any new job, there is generally a person or group of people tasked with showing the ropes to the new hire. Often, the unwritten rules come under the heading of "How to Get Along around Here." The unwritten rules exist because everyone either agrees with them or feels compelled to behave in compliance with them. The idea that the way things are done around here is a shared notion is key to understanding nonprofit culture.

Organizational culture is also reflected in the way newcomers are selected to become a part of the institution, whether the newcomers are new staff, administrators, volunteers, or board members. Once the newcomers have accepted the invitation to join the nonprofit in whatever capacity, what they are told about the nonprofit and how they are shown the ropes of routine institutional life is a reflection of organizational culture. Some nonprofits are very open about how decisions are made, how ideas can bubble up, and how grievances are settled.[6]

Organizational Culture and Behavior   Probably the most powerful illustration of how an organization's culture works is in the types of behaviors that are either rewarded or have no consequences imposed. Even more importantly, what types of behaviors are either punished or extinguished? The terms *reward* and *punishment* here are not to be taken as entirely positive or negative. Consider the two words in terms of whether negative consequences are imposed by the institution for engaging in particular behaviors. Staff who do not show up for work and have not called in sick will probably have some sort of consequences imposed for this behavior—reduction of pay for that week, assessing multiple sick days/vacation days, or a letter of reprimand. However, other destructive/negative behaviors such as failing to meet deadlines, failing to comply with new directives, or foot-dragging in terms of SOX best practices might have no consequences imposed.

Conversely, some behaviors are extinguished (i.e. discontinued) because insufficient positive reinforcement has been extended.[7] In other words, if someone completes a task that he or she believes is expected and the results are either ignored or criticized, it is unlikely the person will do it again. Consider the case of a staff member who worked long into the night to complete a report for the next day. If his or her supervisor does not show the requisite level of appreciation, it is unlikely that the staff member will go to those lengths in the future. Whether or not a behavior is repeated is often contingent upon the degree of positive or negative reinforcement applied in immediate response to the behavior. An organization's culture supplies the reinforcing environment, values, beliefs, and applicable resources to either reinforce or extinguish behavior. Every organization has a unique and irreplaceable culture that reflects its human dimension. Why does change occur in an organization? Change occurs because the current methods or solutions don't work for them anymore.

It isn't enough for a board chair to just announce that the nonprofit is embarking on a SOX best practices program; the staff and volunteers need to understand that this is not a passing fad, but a real and lasting change in the way things are done around the nonprofit and what behavioral changes are expected.

Organizational Citizenship

Why do the staff in some nonprofits ensure that the office is kept clean and that visitors are greeted or do other tasks that are not specific to their job descriptions? These actions indicate that the people in the nonprofit are good organizational citizens. Organizational citizenship describes individuals sense of their role within the organization and those expectations that individuals see as their obligation to the organization. Scholars over the years have described organizational citizenship in terms of an extra–role behavior that is not formally recognized or rewarded by the organization.[8]

Individuals' sense of their organizational citizenship obligations can come in the form of small gestures such as making another pot of coffee if they have poured the last cup or emptying the trash.

Do as I Say, Not as I Do

How often have you observed leaders articulating specific ideals and values only to appear to make choices that contradict these ideals? An everyday example of this would be the mother who tells her child that it is important to eat vegetables and fruits, but who never eats vegetables herself. The child would not only find this contradiction confusing but also see it as evidence that there is little value in eating vegetables and fruits.

All nonprofits have values. Some of these values are written down and some are just understood in terms of how things get done around here. What established values do nonprofit leaders embrace? Do they make decisions clearly based on these values? Or are the nonprofit's values given lip service only to have decisions made based on other, shadow values? The nonprofit's values might also be the ones embedded in the nonprofit by its founder. "Mental Models are deeply ingrained assumptions generalizations, or even pictures or images that influence how we understand the world and how we take action."[9] People may not always do as they say, but they take action based on what they believe to be reality.[10] Why? Because the results work for them. That doesn't mean that the results are the right ones for the organization; it just means that the results are working for the decision makers.

Getting in Touch with Your Authentic Organization

So what does all of this mean for your nonprofit? One of the reasons strategic planning is often ineffective is that nonprofits are not in touch with their authentic organization. They are not able to understand its organizational culture or the ways in which problems are identified and solved. Don't dismiss this as New Age babble. The reality is that unless strategic planners fully understand how the nonprofit is *really* structured and how all of the systems and subsystems *really* operate in a type of harmonization, the planners will find strategic planning a very difficult or even impossible endeavor. Strategic planners must fully understand *how* the goals, objectives, and strategies presented in the strategic plan *will actually impact* the organization, how the changes *will actually play out* in the nonprofit, and what the consequences of these changes will be.

The implementation of SOX requirements and best practices will put strategic planners in touch with the authentic organization and help planners identify the ways in which they can activate the plan once it is written.

Is your Nonprofit Dysfunctional?

Most of the time organizational dysfunction isn't something that can be readily identified. The types of problems that occur and the discord that takes place in personal interactions can signal problems. As you observe the activity in a nonprofit, be aware of additional clues that indicate problems.

Clues to Observing Dysfunction

Attitudes and Beliefs   Dysfunctional attitudes and beliefs are often at the root of organizational dysfunction. How often have you heard people in a nonprofit say:

- "We're poor, grassroots, small, not part of the establishment, out in the boonies [or whatever]." The litany of woes goes on forever.
- "No one would investigate us, sue us, or [fill in the action]."
- "We're a nonprofit—we don't have to do all of the things that corporations are expected to do."
- "We work too long and hard as it is. We're not going to do more work."
- "Our staff isn't paid very well. I can't be expected to require high performance from them."
- "She's a board member. She gives of her time and money—we can't ask her to actually *do* anything!"
- "I started this agency and we'll do it my way. I know these clients better than anyone."
- *"We've tried it before. That never works."*

These comments are the tip of the iceberg in terms of organizational dysfunction. Choices are being made based on these beliefs. People in the nonprofit are expected to tailor their actions to conform to these beliefs.

Performance and Productivity   Dysfunction within the organization can also be detected in the quality and quantity of output. How productive are staff members? Are reports and other deliverables produced on time? Are deadlines routinely missed? Documents that are produced in a haphazard and unprofessional manner do not inspire confidence in the nonprofit. More importantly, unprofessionally presented materials suggest that the content could easily be inaccurate, misleading, or simply wrong. In some instances, such as the submission of an IRS Form 990, a sloppy submission could garner unwanted scrutiny and possibly an audit.

Performance issues also relate to interpersonal interactions as well as to preparation of documents. How are clients and/or visitors treated when they enter the nonprofit? Have clients or visitors complained that they were either ignored or treated in a callous manner? These types of complaints are not nuisance issues—take these complaints seriously.

Appearance of Premises, Staff, and Volunteers   The old adage "You can't judge a book by its cover" does not necessarily apply to work settings and the individuals who work there. Regardless of the individual's pay status (i.e., employee or volunteer), the nonprofit's credibility is diminished by the presence of individuals whose hygiene and mode of dress suggest that they do not understand that they are working professionals. Nonprofits routinely dismiss this type of dysfunction with the ridiculous excuse that professionally attired staff would be upsetting to its clientele. Don't clients deserve to be assisted by people who care enough to ensure that their appearance is professional?

Similarly, the appearance of the nonprofit's interior and exterior sets the tone for clients and visitors alike. The office housekeeping routine—or lack thereof—can signal serious dysfunction within an organization. If papers are piled high on desks and clutter abounds, that indicates a highly stressed organizational culture and undoubtedly a significant number of errors based on the inability to manage documents.

Interpersonal Behavior and Distress   How do people in the nonprofit treat each other? Body language and other nonverbal cues can provide clues to the source of organizational dysfunction. When the executive director arrives, do people scatter? What about board members? When it is clear to the observer that the arrival of an individual prompts an exit of others, there's a problem.

How do they speak to each other? In dysfunctional organizations, there may be more overt displays of friction, such as staff shouting at each other or at management staff. Tone of voice, use of profanity, and demeaning language are obvious clues of organizational difficulty. Whining or other adolescent-like speech patterns can hint at underlying morale problems, or it can signal a previously successful method of shirking responsibility. The more the staffer whines about being overworked or having no resources or support, the less likely the recipient of the whining will insist on the deliverable.

More often than not, those who staff a dysfunctional organization will employ the default position of why they can't provide the deliverable rather than engage in meaningful discussion to develop a strategy that can deliver the goods. The more excuses, the more dysfunction.

Communication Dysfunction in areas of communication can be observed in the way in which policies and procedures are explained, how changes in external environment are articulated, and how new policies/procedures that relate to current legislation are expected to be implemented.

Because knowledge is power, organizational leaders sometimes hoard whatever bits of information that they have. Fearing that by sharing this information their status within the organization might be compromised, these leaders do their best to ensure that only a select few have access to information. These individuals can go to great lengths to hide away information that has potentially important implications. Obviously, there needs to be a reasonable method for ensuring appropriate security for confidential information, but a culture of unnecessary secrecy in a nonprofit is a huge red flag.

If the environment within the nonprofit is one of secrecy—beware. Also beware of the gatekeepers who guard the secrets, as these individuals are tasked with and rewarded for their unwavering attention to keeping secrets secret.

Finance and Financial Management Internal controls, the preparation and presentation of financial reports, and overall quality of financial management are important indicators of organizational function. Dysfunctional organizations have either sloppy or nonexistent policies and procedures for the management of revenues, payables, donations, and grants.

Lack of Internal Controls Many nonprofit executives and board members believe that the application of internal controls applies exclusively to finance and financial operations. Internal controls are necessary for the effective functioning of the board, human resources, information technology (IT), operations, and administration. The absence of internal controls is not only evidence of sloppy methods; it is also emblematic of a culture that does not have standards or accountability. Not surprisingly, such a culture has a high probability of dysfunction if for no other reason than that of lack of accountability.

Information Technology   The way in which technology is used, misused, or ignored can signal dysfunction within a nonprofit. One of the most common examples of dysfunction is the failure to stay current and to recognize that technology is an integral part of the internal control infrastructure. Sadly, many nonprofits fail to understand the degree to which they depend on technology. It isn't just computers! The term *technology* relates to other important operational tools such as software, hardware, laptops and notebooks, personal digital assistants (PDAs), cell phones, voice mail, e-mail, and Internet access. Failure to adequately manage this array of technology can not only indicate organizational dysfunction; it can also indicate a serious risk to the nonprofit in the form of hackers; theft of confidential data; identity theft; potential for harassment of staff, donors, or others; and other liability scenarios for the organization.

Development and Fund-Raising   The manner in which a nonprofit chooses to raise funds for its continuing operation has the potential to show a positive or negative image to the donors and community at large. Organizational dysfunction can be evident in the manner in which a fund-raising campaign is structured and executed. The quality of customer service that donors or patrons receive is also indicative of the degree of functioning within a nonprofit.

The quality of the overall planning and execution of a fund-raising campaign can indicate levels of dysfunction within the organization. One example that became a public relations soap opera was a West Coast zoo's naming contest for two grizzly bears. The contest was initially open to the public. Then the zoo decided to auction off the naming rights and pay off those public entries with free tickets to the zoo. Then the zoo's management decided that the winners of the auction really didn't get to name the bears, and then happily the couple who won the auction had the sense to ask the zoo to open the naming contest to the public. The fiasco went full circle![11]

Human Resource Management Human resource management holds many clues to the nature of organizational dysfunction. One of the most obvious indicators of organizational dysfunction is a permissive atmosphere that highlights a sense of entitlement on the part of the staff and volunteers. Staff and volunteers are habitually late, frequently call in sick, dress in an unprofessional manner, and do not produce quality work. Staff and volunteers are permitted to treat clients and visitors alike in a disinterested fashion or even with outright hostility. Volunteers are not trained or supervised. The nonprofit fails to appropriately screen paid and volunteer staff for sensitive work and handling confidential materials.

Another sign of organizational dysfunction is the volume of complaints regarding hostile work environment, sexual harassment, or other dysfunctional behavior. Are there complaints about food or other personal items being stolen? Are office spaces orderly or piled with paper and trash? Do staff members treat the nonprofit's furniture, equipment, and other materials with respect?

What is the tone of the furnishings inside staff members' work spaces? The furniture may be provided by the nonprofit, but personal items including pictures, posters, slogan buttons, and other signs can express—sometimes unmistakably—the disdain that the staff member has for the organization, a boss, or other targets within the nonprofit.

Public Trust Public trust is one of the most important assets that a nonprofit has, and at the same time it is one of the most elusive. Public trust isn't something that can be shown to staff, clients, donors, or even members of the public. This fragile and subtle feature is the life breath of a nonprofit organization (private-sector companies are very concerned about their public image as well). But like the life breath that sustains life itself, once it is compromised, the living organism is either damaged or dies. Nonprofit companies that experience scandals or other crises do not always return to normal operation. Those nonprofits that fail to have a crisis communication plan or fail to be transparent or exhibit resentment of public inquiries about financial records are showing signs of dysfunction.

Legal Issues Dysfunctional organizations often either have no under-standing about the significance of legal issues or engage in games of denial to justify their ignorance. Legal issues can relate to required filings such as IRS

Forms 990, workers compensation claims, complaints to regulatory agencies regarding harassment or hostile environment claims, or even failing to understand the connection between the quality of internal controls and legal obligations.

Legal documents such as contracts, leases, filings with state and federal regulators, and licenses need to be secured in an orderly fashion. Dysfunctional organizations often fail to have a coherent filing system that provides quick access to documents when needed.

Many dysfunctional nonprofits do not understand how and why complaints can escalate into litigation. The likely root cause of litigation is that the aggrieved party was either ignored, their allegations dismissed as trivial, or they were treated with disrespect. Nonprofit management may not understand the techniques that can be employed to de-escalate a situation. In today's litigious environment, it is important for nonprofits to fully understand how to protect themselves from spurious claims.

Inability to Understand the Business World   Keeping pace with current legislative and industry trends is more important than ever. The external environment is fraught with change, and this change is unlike that ever witnessed before. In the wake of Enron and other corporate scandals, the federal government is under pressure from the public to crack down on private- and nonprofit-sector abuses. Shareholder activism has paved the way for a new type of activism—donor activism, which demands the same type of transparency from a nonprofit as a shareholder would expect from a corporation. The equivalence of these expectations is unprecedented. Never before have public-sector expectations of nonprofits been so closely aligned with expectations of the private sector.

Organizational dysfunction is evident in the failure to stay current with legislative changes, changes in public expectations and those of important stakeholders such as funders, and failure to stay current with industry issues. Denial of the importance of environmental scanning results in the failure to have everyone in the nonprofit stay current on these issues and engage in routine professional development.

The Board   Today's expectations of nonprofit's boards go beyond simply the governance function. Today's boards are expected to be the head, heart, mind, and conscience of the nonprofit itself. Dysfunction at the board level has a toxic trickle-down effect that will stymie implementation of SOX requirements and best practices and derail even the best strategic plan. Of course, no board is perfect, but how can you tell if your nonprofit's board is seriously dysfunctional?

Some examples of dysfunction in board structure and function include:

- *Attendance at board meetings is uneven.* When board members do not attend meetings regularly, they are not contributing to the board's governance obligations.

- *Senior management runs the board meetings, and discussion is dominated by a few board members.* This symptom of dysfunction seeks to keep the decision making in the hands of a select few.

- *The board meetings are highly choreographed, but the content of the agenda is superficial, including endless reports by senior management.* This dysfunction is another version of keeping the decision making in the hands of a select few.

- *Information on executive compensation packages is kept secret from all but the executive committee.* Keeping this information from the board at large is now illegal for some nonprofits in the state of California. It is also contrary to today's higher levels of expectation for board accountability and transparency.

- *Conflict is either suppressed or used endlessly to block business from being conducted.* This level of dysfunction signals serious problems for a nonprofit board.

- *The board does not have a vision or strategic plan for moving the nonprofit ahead.* Senior staff actively blocks strategic planning. Strategic planning is essential to all nonprofits. Boards that are reluctant to actively engage in strategic planning and replace management who block the efforts are not living up to their fiduciary obligations.

- *Board members have been in place for over five years.* All boards need to have *and enforce* term limits. There is no excuse for board members to remain seated on a board for extended periods of time.

- *The board does not have directors and officers insurance and/or employment practices liability insurance.* Failure to have adequate insurance is a breach of the board's fiduciary obligations.

Modeling the New Behavior: SOX Best Practices

The nonprofit's senior management has the opportunity to present the ways in which the nonprofit will address SOX best practices, but also has the opportunity to show their commitment to the process of SOX best practices and to its outcomes. One of the most effective ways of modeling new behavior is for the nonprofit's senior management to discuss some of the ways in which they have adopted SOX best practices techniques and practices. Not only is this particularly instructive, as it illustrates how SOX best practices techniques and practices apply within nonprofit operations, but it also demonstrates a commitment to SOX best practices.

The nonprofit's management might also consider the technique known as social marketing as a means by which informal leaders within the staff, volunteers, and other stakeholders promote SOX best practices. Social marketing has a side benefit of providing practical illustration of how SOX best practice works within a distinct function of the nonprofit or how it works in a cross-disciplinary manner.

Change is a scary thing for many people. Generally, organizational culture is reinforced through the application of rewards for desired behavior, and consequences for behavior that needs to be modified or extinguished.

The use of rewards and/or consequences in reinforcing the significance of SOX best practices centers on the inclusion of a SOX best practices performance standard in every staff member's performance standards for the upcoming year or marking period. Staff and volunteers will need to meet or exceed expectations on this performance standard to qualify for salary increases or other rewards. However, the most visible means by which the importance of SOX best practices can be demonstrated is by the change of behavior and/or focus by senior management and governance within the nonprofit.

Change Takes Time   Change in any organization takes time, but change does not mean waiting forever. Once the nonprofit's staff, volunteers, and other stakeholders see that SOX best practices are not a fad, not a glitzy trend, that they are part of a better way of doing business, and that there are rewards for practicing SOX best practices, they will begin to adapt it into their routine. The important thing is to keep presenting material to educate about SOX best practices. Reinforcement of the message and illustration of how SOX best practices work in real life and the real life benefits that they brings is what will bring about lasting change.

NEXT STEPS

Chapter 6 begins the discussion of strategic planning by describing the process of planning. Chapter 7 presents a streamlined method for writing a strategic plan using a simple template. Chapter 8 presents ideas for leveraging your nonprofit's SOX best practices and strategic planning.

NOTES

1. Senge, Peter. 1990. *The Fifth Discipline*. New York: Doubleday Currency, p. 154.
2. Id., pp. 9–10.
3. Feder, Barnaby J. 2005. "Peter F. Drucker, a Pioneer in Social and Management Theory, Is Dead at 95." *New York Times,* November 12.
4. Schein, Edgar. 1992. *Organizational Culture and Leadership*, 2nd ed. San Francisco: Jossey-Bass.
5. Id.
6. Jackson, Peggy M., and Toni E. Fogarty. 2006. *Sarbanes-Oxley and Nonprofit Management*. Hoboken, N.J.: John Wiley & Sons, p. 50.
7. See note 4.
8. Holmes, Sarah A., Margaret Langford, O. James Welch, and Sandra T. Welch. 2002. "Associations between Internal Controls and Organizational Citizenship Behavior." *Journal of Managerial Issues*, vol. XIV, no. 1 (Spring).
9. Senge, p. 8.
10. Argyris, C. 1982. Reasoning, Learning and Action: Individual and Organizational. San Francisco: Jossey-Bass.
11. Jackson and Fogarty, pp. 52–59.

Strategic Planning

THE PROCESS

INTRODUCTION

In the last chapter we learned about the psychology of organizations, how organizations learn, and why organizations are sometimes dysfunctional. Although it may seem something of a challenge to "get in touch with your authentic organization," the intent was for readers to think—*really think*—about how their nonprofit identifies problems, gets things done, and shows newcomers "the ropes" (i.e. how to behave and survive within the organization).

Why should your nonprofit care about any of this? Effective and productive strategic planning is contingent on knowing and understanding how your nonprofit works. This basic knowledge is central to the strategic planning team's ability to craft a road map to the nonprofit's next goals. By understanding how things really work—and why sometimes things don't work—the nonprofit can design ways to change behaviors if necessary and to introduce new ideas and methods.

In this chapter, we examine the process of strategic planning from the assembling of a strategic planning team to reflecting on what should be discussed in your strategic plan and preparing for the actual writing and execution of the plan. Remember: Your strategic plan is just a pipe dream unless you have fully engaged in the process of planning.

This chapter also describes how the implementation of SOX requirements and best practices can serve to facilitate an accelerated yet highly effective approach. Emphasis will be placed on the basic utility of a strategic plan and how the process works in terms of defining strategic planning and developing and deploying a strategic plan.

The term *process* often conjures up images of endless meetings in which, after all was said and done, there was more "said" than "done." The process that will be presented here is an active process in which the focus will be on the action, on timelines, and on deliverables. Any effective and well-thought-out process begins with a strategic planning team.

THE PROCESS AND THE STRATEGIC PLANNING TEAM

The nonprofit's strategic planning team needs to really understand the process of strategic planning and how the nonprofit's implementation of SOX requirements and best practices has set the stage and served to forward the action toward strategic planning. For this discussion your planning team needs to understand *process* in terms of implementing an efficient method for strategic planning—one that works for your nonprofit.

If someone were to ask the strategic planning team to describe the form and function of a strategic plan, how would they respond? Would they say that a strategic plan is a wish list or a road map or one person's fantasy? Among the many reasons why nonprofits waste copious amounts of time, money, and labor on strategic planning is that the strategic planning committee does not understand the *process* of strategic planning. The planning process should render what the strategic plan is about, why it is an important element in the nonprofit's sustainability, and *what is expected* in terms of execution of the plan.

The Strategic Planning Committee

Like any good team, your nonprofit's strategic planning committee needs to have the right players. Who are the people who would be good strategic planners in your nonprofit? Strategic planning committees need to be staffed by the nonprofit's "star" players who have exhibited a dedication to teamwork, meeting deadlines, and focusing their energies on deliverables. Sound impossible? Not really, if they are given the support and focus that they need, including perhaps some assistance with their other obligations.

Appointment to the strategic planning committee should be done by the board's executive committee in conjunction with the nonprofit's executive director. The appointment to this committee needs to be perceived as a status assignment. The strategic planning process, if done well, need not take up an extensive amount of time, but for the time that it does take, the committee members should be supported in their other tasks so that they can focus on the task of strategic planning.

The strategic planning committee should represent every facet of the nonprofit from the board to the volunteers to finance, development, programs, and administration. The committee should be large enough to delegate tasks, but not so large as to make discussion and deliberation cumbersome. Above all, the strategic planning committee chair should have a clear understanding of the nonprofit's long- and short-term goals, organizational resources, and materials that will be necessary to craft a realistic organizational profile. The committee chair should also bring a certain level of experience to the process as well as a task orientation. That means he or she needs to place more emphasis on getting things done, rather than worrying about how everyone feels. That's not to say that the committee chair should be a tyrant. The person simply needs to be able to set discussion boundaries, assertively manage the meeting agenda, and *get things done.*

THE STRATEGIC PLANNING PROCESS

Effective strategic planning is a method that rationally evaluates the nonprofit's current resources, programs, human capital, and competitive position to determine the course that it must take as an organization to grow, expand, change course, or embrace a new operational dimension. The process brings together a team of important players within the nonprofit to examine where the organization is now, what it has to work with, and where it is going—and why. It is a rational, grounded exercise that captures the essence of where the organization has been, where it is now, and what its future will look like.

Effective strategic planning *never* engages in magical thinking, nor does it develop plans without taking into consideration the resources necessary to carry out the plans as well as a plan for obtaining the necessary resources. Effective strategic plans always have strategies and tactics assigned to facilitate achievement of goals. Deliverables are assigned and individuals are held responsible for completion of specified elements of the plan.

The Elements of a Strategic Plan

One of the many challenges that strategic planning committees face when attempting to create a strategic plan is deciding what should be in the plan. A simple guideline for the structure of the strategic plan should be to include what is necessary and sufficient. Less is more, but it also needs to be enough. An effective strategic plan has several important elements, as discussed next.

Organizational Profile   The organizational profile presents an overview of the current operations, statistics, and other facts related to the history of the nonprofit. Because strategic planning should examine what the organization knows about itself, the information that the organization gathers over a specific time frame can offer insight into trends, the degree of success that the nonprofit's programs are enjoying, and the areas in which the nonprofit is not enjoying as much success or where the nonprofit has stalled in its efforts.

Before the strategic planning team begins any deliberations, it needs to develop a current profile of the organization. This profile is the essential foundation to strategic planning because it presents important information on the current status of the nonprofit; how it has matured over the years; and the structure of its programs, finances, human resources, and the like. The profile needs to include important data that would provide the reader (who might also be evaluating the organization for funding purposes) with an idea of how programs have grown over the years, how the client base has grown or changed, how the staff has become more professionalized, how the organization has gone about recruiting board members over the last three to five years (or why they haven't), how the financials have grown, how the number of grants and major donations have grown, and how the organization has benefited and become more efficient by means of the implementation of SOX best practices and requirements.

The sources of data include the statistics that the organization gathers on its programs, financial reports, development reports, volunteer statistics, and other measures of the nonprofit's operations. The data can also include auditor's reports and/or recommendations for improvement of systems or internal controls. The strategic plan has to be neutral in the types of data presented—good or bad. The data has to reflect what is *real*.

Sources of information for the organizational profile. As you develop your nonprofit's organizational profile, it is important to examine the information that comes from a number of internal reports. Reports such as the nonprofit's annual report, its IRS 990 forms, previous strategic plans (even if they aren't very good), reports prepared for foundations and public-sector agencies, and reports that are for other sources such as high-wealth donors or potential donors. Examining these reports is important because they tell the nonprofit's external stakeholders about the organization. Of course, it is important to ensure that all information is accurate before the reports are distributed, but for the purpose of crafting an organizational profile, it is important to look critically at these reports. Do the reports show a change, even incrementally, of the nonprofit's position and focus? Do the reports illustrate that the nonprofit is growing or changing its direction?

Perhaps the reports illustrate that the need for one or more of the nonprofit's services or programs has changed. The world changes, people's priorities change, the nonprofit's focus changes. These are important factors that need to be carefully examined. Despite what many nonprofit executives and board members believe, eleemosynary, or charitable, organizations do indeed operate in a competitive environment. They compete for donations, grants, contracts with private-sector agencies, and other types of revenue sources such as retail arrangements as well as professional talent, board talent, and sometimes volunteer talent. Are your programs meeting a need in the community? Are your programs duplicated in other nonprofits? If so, your nonprofit might consider reexamining its programmatic agenda.

The organizational profile serves as a type of "road map" that shows the organization where it is now and helps to establish the parameters for the direction it intends to take.

The organizational profile needs to be comprehensive but still focus on what is necessary and sufficient. A well-crafted organizational profile *is not* a data dump. The information presented needs to serve as a logical framework from which future goals, objectives, and strategies will be crafted. The nonprofit needs to begin designing its move to the next level by clearly describing where it is right now and what internal and external factors will shape where it wants to go and how it will get there.

Environmental scanning. Environmental scanning is a description of the method used to identify factors in the competitive environment in which the nonprofit is operating. All organizations including nonprofits operate in a *competitive environment.* Although most nonprofits do not engage in "sales" of products or investments per se, any time the nonprofit solicits donations or submits a proposal to a foundation or a high-wealth individual, the nonprofit is really pitching its good image and what it does as a reason for the donor to "invest" in the organization. Similarly, many nonprofits vie for contracts with public-sector agencies or for public dollars designated for a specific cause such as AIDS. A review of any foundation's IRS Form 990 will tell a great deal about the foundation's philanthropic focus and the types of organizations that received grants over the last year. Of course, since Forms 990 are public information, it is easy enough to review those of organizations who received the grants to review their organizational profiles.

Other types of information that can be gleaned by environmental scanning include:

- *The local, state, and national economic conditions and forecasted trends.* Has your region been in the throes of an economic downturn? If so, this may signal difficulty in raising funds for a capital campaign or other big-ticket fund-raising drive.

- *Trends in philanthropy.* Environmental scanning can identify philan-thropic trends, particularly if there are similarities in the types of giving from foundations and high-wealth individuals. The trends might also point out programmatic expectations, such as the use of a business plan in proposals or more sophisticated integration of technology in operations.

- *Trends in nonprofit management.* This is an important area to review as part of environmental scanning. For example, trends in litigation against nonprofits are important to know, particularly the court rulings in the matters. Nonprofit scandals and the possible impact these might have on your nonprofit's funding are important to know, particularly if your organization relies on United Way funding, for example. Trends involving the legislative environment and new laws/regulations that affect nonprofits should definitely be examined by your nonprofit's strategic planning committee.

The results of this research will assist the strategic planners in under-standing the philanthropic trends in their area and the programmatic needs.

Successful programs are rewarded by continual funding. The perspective of possible sources of funds is critical to the development of an effective strategic plan, as your nonprofit will want to have discussions with possible funders once the strategic plan is completed. Possible funders include public-sector agencies that might offer contracts or are regulators, foundations, high-wealth individuals, banks, insurance companies, vendors, and other nonprofits with which your nonprofit would partner.

Analysis of the organization's strengths, weaknesses, opportunities, and threats. This type of analysis is known as a SWOT analysis. Many nonprofits have difficulty figuring out where to start the discussion of their strategic planning. A SWOT analysis identifies the nonprofit's strengths, weaknesses, opportunities, and threats. It should take place at the beginning of the strategic planning process because it is a useful method for facilitating a working description of the nonprofit's current operational status and competitive position.

Because the results of the analysis are not written in stone and should be viewed as tentative, the strategic planning committee should be encouraged to look back at the results at specific intervals to either revise or revisit the results. The analysis should be timed in that the discussion for each of these areas should be limited to perhaps 20 minutes or less. All ideas should be accepted at least for the first round. Because the results will be viewed at regular intervals during the planning process, there will be opportunities to refine the results.

Examples of the results of a SWOT analysis. Here are some examples of what a SWOT analysis might render for a nonprofit:

Strengths

- *Good name in the community.* Your nonprofit is well respected in your community.
- *Programs subscribed to capacity.* Your nonprofit has programs that have either few or no vacancies. Clients come to your nonprofit seeking assistance.
- *Collaborate with other nonprofits to serve diverse communities.* Your nonprofit readily works with other nonprofits to offer creative solutions.
- *Owns the building.* Your nonprofit owns at least one of the facilities from which it operates.

Weaknesses

- *Donations have been on a steady downward track.* Your nonprofit's donor base has either remained flat or declined.

- *Board is ineffectual.* Your nonprofit's board does not produce the level of leadership or policy making that is needed in the nonprofit.

- *Auditor has mentioned weakness of financial controls.* In your nonprofit's last audit, the auditor mentioned weaknesses in the organization's financial controls.

Opportunities

- *Another nonprofit would like to partner with your nonprofit to expand programming.* Your nonprofit has been approached by another organization to collaborate on a new community program.

- *Another type of service is needed in the community, and no other nonprofit is providing this service.* The city council has set aside funding to deal with this need and is looking to contract out service delivery. Your nonprofit has an opportunity to propose a contract with the city to provide this service.

- *The empty building next door has been for sale for a year and the seller just reduced the price by 25 percent.* Your nonprofit could purchase this building, providing it can leverage its current financial resources to obtain the financing.

Threats

- *This is the third year of a three-year foundation grant to offer a specific program, and the foundation has not committed to renewing the funding.* Your nonprofit could find that the foundation has decided not to renew the funding for this type of program.

- *The nonprofit's donor base has not been updated in five years. There is virtually no effort to cultivate major donors. The board refuses to engage in any kind of fund-raising.* This threat corresponds to the weakness describing the nonprofit's current fund-raising. The donor base and board involvement are two crucial components in effective revenue generation.

- *The nonprofit's current range of programming is so successful that at least three other nonprofits have adopted programs much like these.* Imitation is the sincerest form of flattery, but having this type of competition is not good for your nonprofit.

The analysis should render some ideas and possible directions for the strategic planning committee. It's important not to take the first "cut" of the analysis as the final word. Although the initial takes on these aspects can render some important disconfirming data, the committee needs to also consider the SWOT results in light of the data that has emerged from the nonprofit's operations and data from environmental scanning.

Description of the nonprofit's operational vision. The purpose of an operational vision is to help a nonprofit reflect on its future in terms of (1) what it wants to become or to dramatically change and (2) how these goals can be achieved within a specific timeline. An important guideline about operational vision is: "*No pie in the sky allowed!*" Visions for the future are real and measurable, make sense for the organization's structure, and contain the type of metrics (measures of success) that lend themselves to rigorous analysis. Strategic planning is a disciplined, organized way of describing your nonprofit's current operational, strategic, and competitive position for the purposes of planning where it wants to go and *how it will get there*. If your nonprofit has no idea how it will achieve a specific goal, then it needs to do more work and research to determine *exactly what steps it must take to achieve the goal*.

Review of current organizational resources. The discussion of organizational resources should be a detailed analysis of those resources—financial, human, and operational—that can be leveraged to begin the journey to the next level. An important section in the strategic plan is the discussion of the nonprofit's current resources. These resources can be financial, specialized skills, intellectual capital, competitive advantage, fixed assets, or any other resources that can be leveraged to hasten the strategic goals. The strategic planning team needs to map out the current areas of resources within the organization. This process may take some brainstorming and some reflection within a reasonable time frame.

Strategic Goals   Having a strategic plan does not give the nonprofit license to plan without ever intending to execute! The document is not intended to be a wish list for the review and approval by the cosmos, nor is it a wish list for the nonprofit's larger donors. Even though the strategic plan could be used to illustrate where the nonprofit intends to go, the driving forces that will get it there are the hard work and persistence of the organization's human capital.

Resources Needed   Where do you want to go, and why do you want to go there? As the strategic planners answer those questions, they need to also be clear about the types of resources that the nonprofit needs to get to the next level. Resources can include people (intellectual capital and unique skill sets), money, buildings, equipment, and strategic partners. Be sure to include a description of where your nonprofit's branch of the industry is headed or a description of a new "niche" area of need that has emerged.

Action Plan and Timeline, Deliverables and Accountabilities   The strategic plan also needs a section that describes the action steps that the nonprofit needs to take within a specific time frame to achieve its stated goals. The action plan needs to be very clear about the types of deliverables that are expected at every stage of the plan and identify those individuals who are directly accountable for the deliverables.

Strategic Planning Blunders   Although there are really no right or wrong answers when engaging in strategic planning, there are missteps. Whatever you do, beware of wandering down these paths:

- *Magical thinking.* What is magical thinking? If the strategic planners cannot give a rational explanation of *how* the nonprofit will achieve its strategic goals, obtain the resources that it needs to achieve these goals, or where the money is coming from, then it is engaging in magical thinking. Do not engage in magical thinking.

  Here are some samples of magical thinking:
  - Listing the proposals that have been submitted for funding along with the sums requested and making it look like that much money has been committed by the funders.
  - Resting on the organization's previous accomplishments as reasons for why the organization will be funded.
  - Asserting that "the cosmos, universe, or other higher power will provide." When have you *ever* heard anyone in the private sector make such an assertion in identifying the source of capital? Yes, a

higher power or the universe or whatever your organization's spiritual source is called does indeed provide many resources and may very well inspire others to give. For the purposes of strategic planning, the *specific sources* of funding or revenue that your plan identifies must have some type of tax status with the IRS. Even if your nonprofit is a faith-based organization, good stewardship of its funding dictates that it is to operate as a business. It is simply not acceptable to draft a strategic plan that has goals and outcomes, but does not specify how the organization plans to go about securing the resources and capital necessary to bring the plan to fruition.

- *Deficit budgets.* No deficit budgets—ever! Equally destructive is the construction of a budget that "looks" balanced but is predicated on a level of revenue that the nonprofit is unsure of how it will obtain, or cannot provide a rational explanation for why the revenue is likely to be obtained.

- *Failure to include alternative plans.* The strategic planning team needs to ensure that a significant part of the process focuses on identifying the primary, secondary, and tertiary sources of funding. Never allow the strategic plan to be put into jeopardy because "Plan B" or "Plan C" was not written to identify other strategies for obtaining the necessary funding.

How Should Strategic Planning Work?

It is important to note that strategic planning is *not* an endless SWOT analysis, nor is it a plan that the organization never intends to execute. Strategic planning, if properly managed, does not have to take forever, nor does it plan for the next five years. The private sector's strategic planning envisions 18-month horizons. That's very reasonable in today's fast-paced business environment. Like it or not, your nonprofit *is* a business, albeit one with a unique tax status, but a business nevertheless. Foundations and public-sector agencies expect nonprofits to submit proposals for funding that look like business plans because they *are* business plans.

Strategic Business Plan   Business plans describe the goals and objectives of the operations along with the necessary strategies needed to achieve the objectives and, hence, the goals. Business plans also describe the resources, financial capital, intellectual capital, equipment, real estate, and other resources needed to achieve the goals. The description of the resources needs to be *accurate,* meaning that the writers of the plan cannot lowball the projected cost just because they are afraid the board will reject it. Nor should the writers deny that the plan will not come to fruition without hiring highly skilled individuals to contribute various aspects of intellectual capital. The days of keeping on "dead wood" because they have given so many years of service to the nonprofit for so little pay are *over.* Your nonprofit needs to make the tough decisions in an unflinching manner.

Business plans also take the next step in describing, via a projected budget, the *sources* of funding, skill sets (i.e., how many people with specific skill sets will need to be hired), and how much it will cost to manage the venture. One of the primary reasons why so many nonprofit strategic plans are "nonstarters" is that the writers of the plans simply do not (or will not) take responsibility for laying out the plan in terms of *all of the necessary resources*. Financial resources are just one aspect of the business plan. The business plan:

- *Should be the next step after implementation of SOX requirements and best practices.* Capture the momentum of action and awareness that comes from a dedicated period of time for "housecleaning" and implementation of SOX requirements and best practices. Keep up the message that the old ways of doing business are no longer acceptable.

- *Should be top-down in terms of support and understanding of the current organizational status and where the organization is headed.* Don't bother even starting a strategic plan without the *up-front and visible* commitment from the nonprofit's board and executive director. Everyone in the organization needs to know that the strategic planning process is sanctioned from the highest levels of the organization. What's even more important is ensuring that this visible level of support remains once the planning document is completed and the implementation phase begins.

- *Should have procedures in place to communicate the results of the planning to everyone in the organization and to important external stakeholders.* Chapter 8 provides more information on strategies to ensure that the results of the planning are known and leveraged.

- *Should have deliverables, deadlines, accountability, and consequences for failing to perform.* Along with presenting accurate financials, this is one of the most challenging aspects of strategic planning for nonprofits.

- *Must be executed—ACTION!!*

This aspect of the strategic planning process may be particularly challenging for the strategic planning team. Several things need to be happening at the same time. The plan has been approved by the board, so now it needs to be publicized. Some nonprofits even go so far as to put the strategic plan on their web site. It is particularly important to ensure that everyone in the organization knows the salient points of the plan and the role that each will have in moving the nonprofit to the next level. The strategic planning committee will also need to take steps to execute the plan. Chapter 7 will present a more detailed map of the process. Some of the areas that the committee will need to address include:

- Examining current organizational structure and programmatic agenda to determine how the structure and programmatic offerings might have to change. What must be done to get there?

- What "homework" has to be done in terms of strengthening the organization, repositioning resources, pruning "dead wood," revitalizing the nonprofit's "brand," and examining the effectiveness of current programs. What resources would be needed to do this?

- What changes in the organization and organizational culture would have to be accomplished to meet the goals articulated in the strategic plan?

- Explain how organizational culture can be modified to meet new goals.

Action Steps

The strategic planning committee needs to ensure that they have developed a complete and integrated map of action steps along with the necessary metrics to track successes. Chapter 7 addresses these important next steps to be implemented as soon as the plan is written:

- Establish solid strategies to sequence the actions, articulate the deliverables, and assign responsibilities.

- Structure to hold people accountable and to create effective interventions to keep the process moving toward the goals.

- Establish "mile markers" to determine if the process is on track and to implement midcourse corrections to address any problems or obstacles.

- Assess the effectiveness of the current plan.

An important aspect of the strategic planning process is recognizing that the process takes place along a continuum of time. When strategic planning committees stop or even take a break, the momentum ceases. The private sector learned long ago that in order to get the appropriate return on the investment of time and resources, strategic planning needs to be in continuous motion.

Private-Sector Strategic Planning

Why are private-sector firms successful in designing and executing strategic plans?

- *Private-sector firms understand that the plan is a strategic business plan* and fully intend for the plan to result in raising capital, improving competitive positioning, and aligning resources to launch a new product or other important growth results. Private-sector firms never—ever—create a strategic plan without fully understanding where the sources of capital are, the probability of obtaining first-tier funding, and having a backup plan.

- *Private-sector firms are accountable to their investors.* They have no problem making the necessary course correction to implement the strategic plan. The private sector swiftly holds people accountable for performance and deliverables. They have no problem in pruning "dead wood" and replacing those employees who simply do not perform. They see human capital for what it is—an asset that either needs to deliver results or be replaced.

- *Results, results, and results.* Just as location, location, location is the primary focus of real estate, results are the primary focus of private-sector strategic planning. For example, a high-tech firm needed to standardize production methodologies to decrease cost and increase flexibility. The firm sent the corporate director of software implementation to introduce the standardized production methods and software at each of the facilities. At the first facility, this director received a very cold reception from the plant supervisor, who was not interested in implementing any of these changes. The director contacted his supervisor, the company CEO, who terminated the plant manager the next day. Word spread quickly throughout the firm that senior management was deadly serious about introducing standardization. They understand that success is directly tied to the firm's ability to access and utilize resources—time, financial capital, and intellectual capital.

- *They understand that their investors expect a positive return on investment.* Nonprofit donors, just like private-sector shareholders, expect to see their money used wisely. Unlike private-sector shareholders, nonprofit donors do not expect monetary dividends. They do expect to see that their money is doing good in the community and is being well managed by the nonprofit.

SOX and Strategic Planning

Moving the Nonprofit to the Next Level

Your nonprofit's strategic planning will benefit from SOX implementation because:

- Implementing SOX requirements and best practices establishes a foundation for organizational change and *creates a momentum* that can be leveraged to create an effective strategic plan.

   This type of momentum is often reflected in a more visible discipline to stay on task and the emergence of a level of time management and mission-centered focus that will serve to accelerate the strategic planning process without sacrificing quality or efficiency.

- The implementation process puts management and staff in touch with organizational realities and illustrates how rewards and consequences need to be adjusted to obtain *compliance and results.*

- Internal controls are essential components to ensure financial and organizational stability.

- It is a means of "getting your house in order" prior to embarking on strategic planning.

- It improves competitive positioning because SOX implementation is still relatively rare in the nonprofit world—the more professional a nonprofit becomes, the better its competitive position.

- It establishes and/or strengthens the nonprofit's "brand."

The Continuum of Strategic Planning

Strategic planning isn't simply something that a nonprofit decides to do and then jumps ahead to write. Some nonprofits think that all they have to do is hire a consultant or download a template. That renders a document that your nonprofit could call a strategic plan, but it is as authentic as a photo of an automobile is to the car itself. Both are nonstarters. The implementation of SOX requirements and best practices puts your nonprofit in touch with all of the systems and subsystems that make the organization work. Even if your nonprofit is small, there are still "systems" in place that render the organization's output and delivery. Simply put, strategic planning has a beginning, a middle, and an end—and results! However, without first taking a look at how your organization is designed, what works, and what needs modification, your strategic planning will simply be an exercise in wishful thinking.

The overall plan should be a reflection of the nonprofit's work in SOX requirements and best practices because the results from the SOX implementation serve to shape the nonprofit's current profile and expectations for the future. The strategic plan will capture these expectations and prioritize them in a way that is congruent with the nonprofit's SOX implementation.

NEXT STEPS

The logical next step is to write the plan! Chapter 7 will guide you through a simple template for writing a strategic plan and provide a sample of a strategic plan for the Marywood Thrift Shop and Consignment Boutique.

Writing and Executing the Strategic Plan

INTRODUCTION

In the last chapter we learned about the process of strategic planning and the role that Sarbanes-Oxley requirements and implementation has in preparing the nonprofit to move to the next level. This chapter presents a discussion of the methods used to write a strategic plan, including a sample template designed to streamline the actual writing of a strategic plan. The template includes sections that discuss the nonprofit's organizational and governance profile, strengths, weaknesses, opportunities, threats, environmental findings, and presentation of the nonprofit's future vision and direction.

For many nonprofit managers and board members, the idea of designing, writing, and executing a strategic plan is disheartening because they genuinely fear producing a plan that will be ridiculed or considered substandard. The source of this fear can be the unsettling belief that the organization will not be able to move to the next level or that there is no need to engage in strategic planning. The value of implementing SOX best practices before engaging in strategic planning is that these activities ultimately examine and depict the genuine nature of the organization. SOX best practices not only install essential internal controls, but also provide additional insight into the nonprofit's strengths, weaknesses, and current resources. For these reasons, SOX best practices can serve to accelerate the strategic planning process.

The strategic planning process can also be accelerated by ensuring that everyone on the committee understands the nature of the process, the structure of the strategic plan, the expected deliverables, and the behavioral norms. The issues that we explore in this chapter include:

- Common pitfalls in crafting a plan
- Crafting goals and objectives
- The role of the strategic planning committee
- What the plan should look like
- How long it should take
- The outcomes of the strategic plan
- Executing the strategic plan
- Sample strategic plan for the Marywood Thrift Shop and Consignment Boutique

COMMON PITFALLS: WHY NONPROFITS HAVE TROUBLE WRITING A STRATEGIC PLAN

Nonprofits often have difficulty writing and executing an effective strategic plan because the nonprofit staff and the strategic planning committee don't understand how a strategic plan works or why the organization needs such a plan. Part of the confusion might come from the board's lack of participation, or from inadequate preparation. When the board has not explicitly exerted leadership in designing, preparing for, or executing the plan, then they will have difficulty communicating the purpose of the strategic plan. The entire organization needs to understand the role and value of pre-plan preparation including implementation of SOX requirements and best practices. The strategic planning process can be more productive and facilitated more efficiently by understanding—and avoiding—these common pitfalls.

Pitfall 1. Setting the Agenda from the Top.   The strategic planning purpose and process is not clearly articulated by the board and senior management. The board and senior management need to announce that the nonprofit is about to embark on a strategic planning process. The members of the strategic planning committee should be introduced to the entire organization within the context of their expected contribution to the process. The strategic planning committee is the nonprofit's dream team and should be presented as such. The board and senior management should also make their expectations clear to the strategic planning committee in terms of vision, available resources, and timeline for completion of the first draft of the strategic plan.

Pitfall 2. Endless Analysis. The SWOT analysis is an important component in determining the current status of the nonprofit and what opportunities, as well as barriers, will be present as the organization moves forward. As with any tool, the SWOT analysis is intended to capture a moment in time. The SWOT analysis is not intended to present an exhaustive catalog of strengths, weaknesses, opportunities, and threats. Strategic planning committees, in their zeal for perfection or fear of making a mistake, focus far too much time and emotional energy on what should be a viewed as a transient tool.

If the planners become stuck in an endless SWOT analysis, there will be little progress in writing a plan. Your organization's strengths, weaknesses, opportunities, and threats should address all factors that are key to its future success, including your program and client needs, expectations, and opportunities as well as your core competencies, your competitive environment, and your performance relative to competitors and comparable organizations.

Pitfall 3. Lack of Access and Cooperation. The strategic planning committee is not given the level of access and cooperation that is needed to complete tasks or conduct adequate research. Committee members are overburdened by their day-to-day task assignments. The team receives very little cooperation from their colleagues or supervisors.

Complete access to any and all documents, reports, or other materials should be made to at least the committee chair. The chair should have the right to insist on full access and cooperation. Resistance to requests for materials or assistance should be dealt with swiftly. If sufficiently unpleasant consequences are associated with the first instance of this type of behavior, it is unlikely that the behavior will be repeated anywhere else in the organization. The strategic planning process is too important to be delayed by bureaucratic stalling.

Pitfall 4. Nibbling around the Edges. The strategic plan is not evaluated or edited in a meaningful manner by the members of the committee. As the first draft of the strategic plan is evaluated, the committee needs to be explicitly instructed to *focus on substance*. Committee discussion on the placement of bullet points or the type of font used is *not substance*. The committee should be reminded that the document will receive a final, technical edit by a senior administrative assistant who is well versed in fonts and bullet points. The committee is obligated to pay attention to the content. The strategic plan is the roadmap that the organization will be using to move to the next level.

THE ROLE OF THE STRATEGIC PLANNING COMMITTEE

In Chapter 6, we discussed the strategic planning committee's important task in terms of facilitating the design of the strategic plan. The committee is the heart of the process as the team represents the various components of the nonprofit's structure, functions, and priorities. The committee should be large enough to represent the whole of the organization, but not so large that discussion presents a barrier to progress.

The role of the strategic planning committee can be framed in terms of who the members are; what they are expected to do before, during, and after the process; and why they were chosen to serve on this important committee.

Who

Members of the strategic planning committee should represent the most important operational and functional areas of the organization. At least one committee member should represent the organization's financial function, information technology, and development (fund-raising). Depending on the size of the nonprofit, a board member might be chosen to serve, but the member should not be part of the executive committee.

What Are They Expected to Do Before, During and after the Process

The strategic planning committee should be expected to complete pre-planning assignments, attend all meetings, contribute to the discussion in a *meaningful* manner, and produce the deliverables assigned.

Why Were They Chosen

The members of the strategic planning committee were chosen for their star power, as noted in Chapter 6. Appointment to a strategic planning committee should be considered a plum assignment and accorded the requisite level of prestige. A person is invited to join the committee because he or she has demonstrated a high level of strategic thinking, business acumen, and ability to solve problems creatively.

Because of the intense deliberations and need for creative thinking, the team should be permitted to work together initially without outside interference in the form of other job-related deadlines. Support for the strategic planning committee members' workloads needs to be built into the process.

CRAFTING GOALS AND OBJECTIVES

One of the most insidious reasons for problems in writing a strategic plan can stem from the fact that the planners don't ever expect that the plan to be executed. This troublesome mind-set occurs because the planners do not understand how to achieve what they identified as the strategic planning goals. The planners might not fully understand the expected function of a strategic plan or how it can help the nonprofit map out the approach necessary to move to the next level. When planners do not realize that with the changing times comes the expectation of a higher level of profession-alism, their efforts in strategic planning may be cut short. Increasingly, senior management positions in nonprofits of all sizes are being recruited from the private sector. Why? Managers with experience in the private sector understand how to align resources, manage for performance, ensure the financial stability of the organization, and make certain that the nonprofit is in compliance with laws such as Sarbanes-Oxley.

Of course, it's entirely possible that nonprofit strategic planners might have difficulty writing a plan because they do not have a template to use for their initial draft and they do not know how to execute the plan. Later on in the chapter we examine the use of a strategic planning template and how the plan can be executed in a structured, organized manner.

Goals need to describe what the next level looks like. They should depict the final outcome of the strategic planning process. As mentioned earlier, the nonprofit's mission is the compass that guides the organization. Goals need to be consistent with the nonprofit's mission as well as indicate how the strategic plan will change the organization. Organizational change must still be harmonious with the mission.

Objectives describe the elements that must be in place to support achieving the goals. Strategies describe how objectives will be achieved, and tasks are the logical action steps needed to fulfill the strategy.

It is essential to ensure that the strategic goals make sense and describe the direction that the nonprofit wants to take. The goals do not have to be long, elaborate, or poetic prose. They do need to be clear, concise, and doable. Everyone has to agree that the goals can be achieved before the process can continue.

What Should the Strategic Plan Look Like?

Exhibit 7.1 shows the outline of a typical strategic plan table of contents. The explanation for each section appears below each of the headings.

Institutional Profile

The strategic plan should guide the reader in understanding the fundamental elements, values, and vision that empower your nonprofit. From this introduction, the reader should also begin to see how the *process* of strategic planning is an integral part of every level of your nonprofit, from the board to the most basic of operations. It includes the following points:

- **History of the Nonprofit.** This section must be very brief, including only salient points, such as: How does the nonprofit's historical direction support further strategic planning and establish the foundation for the current strategic plan?

EXHIBIT 7.1	STRATEGIC PLANNING TEMPLATE WORKING DRAFT

Table of Contents

Institutional Profile

History of the Nonprofit *(needs to be very brief—only salient points)*

Mission, Goals, and Objectives of the Nonprofit

Summary of Relevant Facts and Statistics

Summary of Results from [the last] Strategic Plan of 2XXX

Strategic Planning Process at the Nonprofit

Strategic Planning and Governance

- Include statement from the board on their commitment to strategic planning as a component of the board's legal and fiduciary obligations and their support of the strategic planning committee.
- Include mention of the board's commitment to remaining in compliance with SOX and any relevant state/local legislation having to do with accountability and transparency.

Strategic Planning Committee

- Members
- Process
- Deliverables for current round of strategic planning
- Ongoing activities and implementation of the action directives from the board
- Evaluation plan and timeline for current results and preparation timeline for next round of strategic planning

Environmental Scan

- Trends in the nonprofit world particularly as these relate to:
  - Significant litigation and court decisions
  - Legislation and regulatory requirements (like the IRS)
- Comparable programs in other nonprofit organizations

Analysis of Nonprofit Strengths, Weaknesses, Opportunities, and Threats

Sample areas for review:

- Governance
- Organizational infrastructure and efficiency (including internal controls)
- Administration and management (quality of productivity and morale)
- Development and fundraising
- Programs—current and future relevance. Are the programs making a difference? How?
- Industry expectations. What's being funded by foundations, major donors and public sector these days?

(continued)

EXHIBIT 7.1   (CONTINUED)

- What opportunities does the nonprofit have to improve its response to the organizational mission? Serve more people? Improve its image and reputation? Attract more donors and build a more solid donor base? Strengthen its financial infrastructure? Build an organization that can withstand any business interruption/ disaster/catastrophe that is tossed its way?
- What are the organization's dreams? How do these dreams correspond to the organizational mission? How are these dreams visualized—can the outcomes be imagined?

Next Level
Where do we want to be? What resources are required? Alignment of resources— current resources and resources that will be needed to move to the next level.

Two- to Three-Year Strategic Goals
Strategic Goals Focus Areas for Next Year

- Results—how the results are moving us forward
- Next level—recommendations and necessary resources
- What opportunities does the nonprofit have to improve its response to the organizational mission? Serve more people? Improve its image and reputation? Attract more donors and build a more solid donor base? Strengthen its financial infrastructure? Build an organization that can withstand any business interruption/ disaster/catastrophe that is tossed its way?
- What are the organization's dreams? How do these dreams correspond to the organizational mission? How are these dreams visualized—can the outcomes be imagined?

Recommendations for Priority Action
This section will break out the key pieces of the plan into goals, objectives, and strategies for the next two to three years. The recommendations will also include clear descriptions of the resources needed to move to the next step—the resources might also include changes in attitudes, behaviors, productivity levels, skill sets, and the like.

- **Mission, Goals, and Values of the Nonprofit**. This section presents the mission, goals, and values of the organization. The mission of the nonprofit is the compass for strategic planning. The mission provides the rationale for moving to the next level and overarching goal for the planning process. The nonprofit's goals and values are the touchstones for the process. Strategic planning is *never* a means by which the organization's mission, goals, and values are compromised or contradicted.

- **Summary of Relevant Facts and Statistics.** The institutional profile should contain relevant facts and statistics to help the reader to understand the current status of the nonprofit's finances, program, staffing and operations. For example, the summary could contain the following types of statistical data:

- ○ *Financial reports.* Balance Sheet, Income Statement, and Comparative financials for the last three years. The section should also include the current budget as well as reports on financial performance in terms of budget versus actual and IRS 990 filings for the past three years.
- ○ *Development and fund-raising reports.* These reports should be summarized to illustrate the various sources of income and the expenses associated with fund-raising and development.
- ○ *Programmatic statistics.* Statistical reports that present salient information on the variety of programs offered by the nonprofit should address client subscription to programs, types and quantity of services provided, volunteer hours, number of miles driven, food distributed, or other measures of programmatic success.

The summary should point to those areas or problems that the strategic plan intends to address.

- ○ *Human capital report.* This report should describe the nonprofit's board, management, staffing and volunteer structure. The discussion should also present relevant information on specialized skill sets, or skill sets that are not yet represented, but will be required in the immediate future.
- • Summary of Results from the previous strategic plan. If this is the first strategic plan your nonprofit has ever written, that's fine. This section applies only if a previous strategic plan is in place. Even if the expected results from the previous strategic planning have not come to fruition, that in itself is a result and needs to be reported.

The Strategic Planning Process   The strategic plan also needs to include a section that describes the rationale for engaging in strategic planning. This section needs to include a discussion of the board's commitment to strategic planning as shown in bylaws, board policies, and/or other documentation. Describe how your nonprofit has established a solid internal control system through the implementation of SOX requirements and best practices. Your nonprofit's SOX implementation should specifically address board accountability and transparency. Your plan should also note the ways in which SOX implementation has raised the level of accountability and transparency within the organization. Have all of the SOX requirements and best practices been put into place? If not, then describe the strategy and timeline for ensuring that all of the requirements and best practices will be in place by the time the strategic plan is fully implemented. Your strategic planning team should build the other SOX requirements and/or best practices into the plan itself. If some elements of the requirements or best practices need to be refined, be sure to include the anticipated timeline for completion.

Strategic Planning and Governance   The board's strategic vision and priorities need to be clearly presented in the nonprofit's institutional profile. As the governance entity of the organization, the board is the rudder that steers the ship. The nonprofit's mission is the compass and the strategic plan is the route that is designed to ensure that the ship does not hit the rocks. The board needs to be clear about its commitment to the process as a component of their legal and fiduciary obligations. The board should describe its vision and priorities for the nonprofit as well as its commitment to support the outcomes of the strategic planning process.

The board should express their support of the strategic planning committee as well as its commitment to remaining in compliance with SOX and any relevant state/local legislation having to do with accountability and transparency.

Strategic Planning Committee   This section of the plan should introduce the members of the strategic planning committee and describe the process that the committee will use in designing the plan and the deliverables for the current round of strategic planning. Stakeholders who will be reading the strategic plan will want to know about important standards such as timeline, assignments, and deliverables. The process for designing the plan should include these important benchmarks:

- *Anticipated timeline.* The timeline will indicate the pace at which planning will take place. In order to leverage the SOX compliance that the nonprofit has put into place, the pace for strategic planning needs to be accelerated. This means that there may be strategic planning committee meetings once or even twice a week.

- *Committee assignments.* The committee members need to be given specific assignments in terms of data gathering, environmental scanning, analysis and the like. Readers of the strategic plan will want to know who was responsible for the statistical reports, analysis, or other task areas.

- *Deliverables.* The deliverables should be described in a fairly general manner, as there are varying levels of deliverables from goal-setting to task assignments to support strategies. The reason that a general discussion of deliverables should be included is to give readers an idea of how the work was divided among committee members, particularly those members with specified skill sets.

- *Is the plan working?* The plan should describe the committee's evaluation strategies and timeline for current results and preparation timeline for the next round of strategic planning

- *What the committee will do if the plan isn't working.* The strategic plan should also contain guidelines for revisiting the overall outcomes and deliverables if the plan does not appear to be rendering the desired outcomes.

Environmental Scan   The environmental scan component of the strategic plan describes the trends in the nonprofit world, particularly as these relate to important legal decisions, legislation and regulatory requirements (like the IRS), and comparable programs in other nonprofit organizations.

Consider developing an environmental scan that is both general (macro) and specific (micro). The macroscan addresses the trends in the nonprofit world. The microscan should examine what is happening in your community, state, and region. For example, a microscan could show what types of programs are being funded by local and regional foundations and how nonprofits offering similar services are generating new revenue streams.

What are the benchmarks for programmatic quality? Your local library and a helpful librarian could assist in finding statistical resources to help the strategic planning committee in establishing benchmarks for service and quality in the type(s) of programs that your nonprofit offers.

SWOT Analysis   Chapter 3 presented an initial discussion of the SWOT analysis and provided samples of nonprofit strengths, weaknesses, opportunities, and threats. As the strategic planning committee engages in a SWOT analysis, consider these areas for review:

- *Governance.* The term *governance* addresses how the board is organized and how well it provides leadership and engages in policy making. The quality of your nonprofit's board's governance should be considered in terms of the value that it adds to the nonprofit's ability to move to the next level.

- *Organizational infrastructure and efficiency (including internal controls).* The nonprofit's organizational infrastructures include internal controls, systems, and other aspects of the operational structure. The implementation of SOX requirements and best practices has already provided a measure of additional strength in your nonprofit's organizational infrastructure.

- *Administration and management (quality of productivity and morale).* How effective is the nonprofit's management? Does the administrative function of the organization manage the day-to-day operations in an efficient manner?

- *Development and fund-raising.* The nonprofit's trend in development and fund-raising need to be considered as part of the SWOT exercise. Based on past results and current human capital, will your nonprofit be able to access the financial resources that it will need to move to the next level?

- *Programs: current and future relevance.* Are your nonprofit's programs making a difference? How are these programs genuinely changing people's lives or the community as a whole? This question addresses the nonprofit's current and future programmatic relevance. However, do not simply rely on indirect evidence such as testimonials from clients. Explore deeper; find out *how* the program is making a difference. Determine the specific learning or specific behavioral changes or specific changes in attitudes that have come from these programs. It is essential that the measure of programmatic strength is coming from solid evidence.

- *Industry expectations.* What's being funded by foundations, major donors, and public sector these days? Some of this information can be found in the environmental scan, but some valuable information can also be obtained in "informational" interviews with key community and business leaders. Members of the strategic planning committee could schedule informational interviews with these important stakeholders to obtain their insight and perspectives.

- *Areas of improvement.* How might the nonprofit improve its response to the organizational mission? Serve more people? Improve its image and reputation? Attract more donors and build a more solid donor base? Strengthen its financial infrastructure? How might the nonprofit build an organization that can withstand any business interruption/disaster/catastrophe that occurs?

- *What are the organization's dreams?* How do these dreams correspond to the organizational mission? How are these dreams visualized—can the outcomes be imagined?

Remember, the results of the SWOT analysis are not written in stone. It is a means by which issues are presented for consideration. Some of the issues identified might be incorporated into the plan itself. Some of the issues might simply be acknowledged as part of the working environment.

The Next Level

Where does the nonprofit want to go? What resources does the nonprofit already have? What additional resources are required? The section of the plan that describes the nonprofit's strategic goals needs to be clear in terms of what the organization is planning to do, how the organization will know when it has reached the next level, and what resources it needs to get there. The strategic plan needs to be clear regarding the nonprofit's current resources and how these can be leveraged to begin the move to the next level. This section of the plan can be very challenging. Many strategic planning committees struggle to articulate a vision for the future of the organization. Equally challenging is the struggle to define and describe how the organization's current resources will be used to leverage access to the additional resources needed to reach the strategic goals. An important aspect of this section of the strategic plan is the description of how the nonprofit generates revenue. It is essential that the nonprofit *tell the truth about where the organization gets its funding.* If the nonprofit doesn't have a solid revenue stream in place, then this must be disclosed in this section of the plan. Does the nonprofit have a solid donor base? If not, then admit that the donor base needs work and build in the commitment to develop a solid donor base as one of the goals of the current strategic planning. Does the nonprofit rely too much on grants or public-sector contracts? Is the organization getting its money's worth in terms of development efforts? The answers to these questions need to be contained in this section.

Two- to Three-Year Strategic Goals   This section of the plan describes what the nonprofit intends to focus on for the next two to three years. The section will describe the opportunities the organization has to serve more people, improve its image and reputation, attract more donors, and build a more solid donor base. The strategic goals that are described in this section will serve as the framework for developing the working objectives, strategies, and tasks that will ensure that *genuine movement* takes the nonprofit to the next level.

Recommendations for Priority Action   The recommendations for priority action encompass the project management model that will break out the key elements of the plan into goals, objectives, and strategies for the next two to three years. The recommendations will also include clear descriptions of the resources needed to move to the next step; the resources might also include changes in attitudes, behaviors, productivity levels, skill sets, and the like. The section on executing the plan elaborates on methods for launching a strategic plan and effective project management.

How Long Should It Take?

The design of a strategic plan does not necessarily lend itself to a prearranged timeline, but it should not be permitted to continue in an endless loop. The project management outline needs to contain specific timelines for deliverables, milestones, and task completion. The more specific the expectations are for the *completion of the strategic plan*, the better the results. It is essential that committee members recognize that the writing of the plan is the idea; until and unless the team can actually share a common vision of the end result, nothing will happen. If the team can imagine what the "next level" looks like, feels like, perhaps even "tastes" like, then the plan is ready to be executed.

The value of having implemented SOX requirements and best practices is that the nonprofit's systems, controls, and current policies have been examined for compliance in terms of SOX values. This level of inquiry has probably generated a momentum that can be further harnessed for strategic planning.

EXHIBIT 7.2   TASK–GOAL CONTINUUM

Outcomes of the Strategic Plan

The plan should render a vision for the future based on the goals, objectives, and strategies outlined in the plan, a clearly defined and articulated path to getting to the next level, and a list of resources that will be necessary to go to the next level. Each of the deliverables is a TASK that should clearly contribute to a corresponding STRATEGY that achieves a specific OBJECTIVE that contributes to the achievement of a GOAL. (See Exhibit 7.2.)

In launching the strategic plan, it is essential to assign tasks and accountabilities. The section on launching the plan provides examples of how the deliverables are managed.

How to Execute an Effective Strategic Plan

Launching Your Strategic Plan

Once the strategic plan is written and approved by the board, the important work of executing the plan begins. The strategic plan is one of the most important projects that any nonprofit will put into place and requires a solid

EXHIBIT 7.3   STRATEGIC PLAN FOR XYZ NONPROFIT

Action Steps and Due Dates

Goal & Due Date	Objective & Due Date	Strategy & Due Date	Task & Due Date	Person Accountable

project management system to ensure the appropriate delivery of tasks and strategies leading up to the fulfillment of objectives and goals.

How does the project actually begin? The first step would be to construct an action plan, which is a timeline identifying milestones and associated tasks/ deliverables essential to the launching *and completion* of any plan. Members of the strategic planning committee need to be assigned to a specific project area. Each member also should be assigned to lead a team designated to manage the specific area of the project. For example, if the strategic plan has five strategic goals and the overarching goal of the construction or acquisition of a new building, the timeline would logically show the initial activities of resource alignment and capital campaign preparation.

What does this look like? (See Exhibit 7.3.)

Each member of the strategic planning committee is assigned to lead a team tasked with delivering a particular goal or set of goals. The team assignments along with due dates are listed in this exhibit. *Staying on track and on task is essential!* Each of the areas includes a due date so that team members can see at a glance how the completion of tasks contributes to achievement of strategies, objectives, and goals. The intent is to maintain focus and to continuously look at the big picture. Focus can be maintained by regularly scheduled in-person meetings, conference calls, web-based conferencing, or other means of regular communication.

Why Do Nonprofits Have Trouble Carrying Out a Strategic Plan?

Now comes the really hard part of strategic planning: taking the action necessary to accomplish the strategic goals. Why do many nonprofits have difficulty achieving strategic goals?

- *They have difficulty making decisions.* The goals that are listed in a strategic plan should be clear and attainable, but will require decisions on how to achieve the goals.

- *They have difficulty making commitments.* Writing a strategic plan is one thing; taking action is quite another. Taking the actions necessary for the desired change requires a solid commitment to seeing the strategic goals completed.

- *They have difficulty holding board members, staff, and volunteers accountable for action and deliverables.* Many nonprofit boards and managers are reluctant to hold people responsible and accountable for performance. This isn't a problem in the private sector. It's very simple: *People who don't produce are replaced.* The private sector views performance in terms of money gained or money lost. If an employee doesn't produce, he or she is losing money for the company. Period.

- *They have difficulty identifying the resources needed and develop strategies for obtaining the resources.* Nonprofits that have difficulty executing a strategic plan also have difficulty identifying the resources that they would need to achieve their strategic goals. They have even more difficulty crafting strategies to obtain the resources.

- *They have difficulty developing a timeline to mark the activities that need to be sequenced and executed to achieve the objectives.* If the nonprofit has difficulty with project management, it will be particularly difficult for their staff to establish a project management design to carry out the goals and objectives of the strategic plan.

- *They have difficulty raising productivity levels and breaking out of the status quo.* The nonprofit would need to raise its overall productivity level, and the board, management, staff, and volunteers would be expected to work harder and faster and produce more. That level of change is not comfortable for many organizations, particularly those with a victim mind-set.

- *They have difficulty thinking outside of the box.* One of the greatest challenges in nonprofit management is finding leaders who are not boxed in by the parameters of the organization. Nonprofit executives who have come from the private sector often have an easier time devising approaches that are innovative.

- *They have difficulty recognizing that the nonprofit is a business and that the nonprofit's strategic plan is a strategic business plan.* One of the most difficult changes for nonprofits to accept today is that they are expected to conduct themselves like businesses. Senator Grassley, Governor Schwarzenegger, IRS Commissioner Everson, and others have described how the Congress, the State of California, and the IRS now expect nonprofits to adhere to the same standards of accountability and transparency that are expected in the private sector.

Avoid These Seven Costly Mistakes

Launching your nonprofit's strategic plan is an exciting time. Your chance of success will improve greatly if you do not make these mistakes.

Mistake 1: The plan does not have a detailed timetable that describes what has to happen when.

Solution: Each of the goals, objectives, and strategies has to be sequenced to ensure that the action taking place and the deliverables created act as a foundation for the next steps. Creating goals and objectives is simply the first part of the process. Carrying out a strategic plan means that the planning committee, board, and senior management are in sync with the overall project management. The process does not stop until all of the strategic goals are achieved!

Mistake 2: The a plan cannot come to fruition because the organization lacks the staffing, financial resources, intellectual capital, Rolodex, board support, mission, networking connections, and *political will* to make it happen. The organization is afraid to change the way it operates because that will step on toes.

Solution: The board, strategic planning committee, and management have to be able to imagine the outcome, "see" what it looks like, and know how the outcome will make the nonprofit a better organization. The plan will outline all of the necessary resources, and identify which ones are in place and how the nonprofit will go about obtaining the rest.

Mistake 3: The nonprofit is stuck in a time warp and doesn't understand how times have changed and why the organization needs to change. Often nonprofits are stuck in a bygone era or in the founder's mind-set about the organization.

What does being stuck in a time warp look like? In the critically acclaimed movie *The Queen*, actress Helen Mirren plays Britain's Queen Elizabeth II, a woman who is baffled by her subjects' outpouring of grief over the death of Princess Diana. She is emotionally stuck in the nineteenth-century paradigm of the monarchy that was shaped by her great-grandmother, Queen Victoria. In her royal arrogance, she steadfastly refuses to allow a royal funeral for the princess because the deceased is technically no longer a member of the family. She is convinced that all the fuss will go away until her prime minister, Tony Blair, informs her that a recent poll showed that 70 percent of her subjects disapproved of her handling of the situation and 40 percent of her subjects wanted to abolish the monarchy altogether. The implications of the poll weren't lost—even on the stubborn queen. Her decision making had centered around how Queen Victoria would have done approached the situation. The bad news that Tony Blair offers her is sufficiently jarring to change her decision-making process. Does your nonprofit make decisions based on a set of assumptions that no longer apply?

Solution: If your nonprofit seems stuck in a time warp, review the environmental scan that was part of your strategic plan. Are other nonprofits engaging in innovative approaches? If so, your strategic planning team may want to have a discussion with your banker, attorney, or insurance professional or a community leader to identify the approaches that it could consider. Your nonprofit needs to ensure that the rationale behind where it is going and how it will get there is based on a realistic assessment of its value in the community and to its clients.

Mistake 4: Inability of management to maintain focus on the implementation of the plan—board and senior management are easily distracted. No one is tasked with and held accountable for coordinating the plan. The plan fails to be managed effectively.

Solution: The effective execution of a strategic plan requires a good project management plan. The strategic plan needs to have a solid timeline associated with every step, every action, and every important milestone. The chair of the strategic planning committee needs to personally commit to ensuring that plan execution stays on track. The individual managing the plan needs to be a member of the board or senior management. This task should *never* be assigned to an administrative or executive assistant. The administrator's position in the nonprofit sends a message about the importance of strategic planning to everyone in the organization. If the plan is being administered by a member of the clerical staff, everyone will have license to ignore it.

Mistake 5: The plan did not accurately represent the resources that the nonprofit had to execute it. In other words, the plan was not realistic in terms of the time, money, staff, and other resources that it would take to execute. For example, if a nonprofit wanted to purchase a building but did not describe what resources it would take to locate the property, secure the funding, maintain the building, or manage the operations of the building, it's highly unlikely that the plan would ever come to fruition.

Solution: Rework the plan to ensure that all of the resources are identified and that the planning includes the action steps necessary to secure the necessary resources. *There is no substitute for accuracy in calculating the necessary resources.*

Mistake 6: The main characteristic of the plan is magical thinking. Sometimes such thinking is cloaked in a spiritual sentiment with statements that a higher power will facilitate the execution of the plan.

Solution: The strategic plan needs to present goals that can be really achieved and resources that are either in place or that can be secured— *really.* All of the assertions in the plan should be backed up by research, financial reports, signed contracts, or other definitive assurances.

Mistake 7: The strategic plan fails because the nonprofit lacks the political will to deal effectively with those individuals or groups that refuse to cooperate.

Solution: The nonprofit's well-being ensures that it will continue to provide services to your clients. The well-being of your nonprofit and your clients trumps any protest made by staff or volunteers. Sometimes the most important part of executing a strategic plan is recognizing that it means changing the way things are done. This may require changing the rewards and consequences or simply clearing the deadwood. However, it is essential that you consult with your legal counsel before making any personnel decisions.

Happily, strategic plans are not written in stone. If it appears that your strategic plan may have contain some of these mistakes, it is never too late to make modifications. As the action steps are being devised, you may need to adjust the plan to ensure that the actions will be effective and that resources will be in place.

Sample Strategic Plan for the Marywood Thrift Shop & Consignment Boutique

Introduction

The Marywood Thrift Shop & Consignment Boutique was founded in 1911 as the primary fund-raising venture of the Marywood Neighborhood Auxiliary. Over the years the Marywood grew from a small storefront to its current operations on the busy Millard Street business corridor.

Last year the Marywood board voted to begin strategic planning for the purpose of increasing revenue and creating an efficiency of operational scale by changing the business model. The board also noted that the implementation of SOX requirements and best practices were critical to the success of the thrift shop and consignment boutique regardless of any future strategic planning. Over the following three months, the Marywood Thrift Shop & Consignment Boutique implemented the two SOX requirements and best practices. The board conducted an internal controls audit to confirm that the appropriate policies and practices were in place. The Marywood Thrift Shop & Consignment Boutique was ready to begin strategic planning.

The strategic plan that follows illustrates Marywood's potential for raising its annual net income significantly through the rearrangement of its retail enterprise.

Note: This sample strategic plan is abbreviated for illustration purposes. Your nonprofit's strategic plan needs to contain all of the information that is necessary and sufficient for your nonprofit's strategic planning purposes.

Marywood Thrift Shop & Consignment Boutique Strategic Plan

Institutional Profile

History of the Nonprofit (List only the salient points. The history should be only one to two paragraphs.)

The Marywood Thrift Shop & Consignment Boutique ("Marywood") was founded in 1911 as the primary fund-raising venture of the Marywood Neighborhood Auxiliary. Over the years the Marywood grew from a small storefront to its current operations on the busy Millard Street business corridor.

Mission, Goals, and Objectives of the Nonprofit

The Marywood Thrift Shop & Consignment Boutique's mission is to help improve the Marywood community by sponsoring after-school programs.

Marywood's goals and objectives for the coming year emphasize raising $500,000 to support the Latchkey Kids after-school program by increasing the revenue from its retail operations.

Summary of Relevant Facts and Statistics

- Last year the combined gross revenue of the Thrift Shop & Consignment Boutique was approximately $300,000.

- The thrift shop is approximately 500 square feet in size. In the past year, the net revenue from the thrift shop operations garnered approximately $100 per square foot or $50,000.

- The consignment boutique is approximately 250 square feet in size. In the past year, the net revenue from the consignment boutique operations garnered approximately $800 per square foot or $200,000.

Financial Reports (This section of the plan summarizes the nonprofit's financial profile. Marywood would include the items listed. The actual financial reports would be presented in the appendix of the strategic plan.)

- A summary of its balance sheets for the last three years

- A summary of sales for the past three years

- A comparison of sales per foot between the thrift shop and the consignment boutique for the past three years.

Summary of Results from Marywood Thrift Shop & Consignment Boutique's Strategic Plan of 2XXX—

(*If the nonprofit has not ever done strategic planning, skip this section.*) This section of the strategic plan addresses the *results* of the previous strategic plan that are relevant to the current plan. The emphasis is on results. If the previous strategic plan did not render any results, then mention that a strategic plan was written and simply identify the goals it presented.)

The Strategic Planning Process at the Marywood Thrift Shop & Consignment Boutique

Strategic Planning and the Board   (This section of the strategic plan describes the board's commitment to the strategic planning and also includes the next items.)

- A statement from the board that members are committed to strategic planning as a part of their legal and fiduciary obligations and that they support the strategic planning committee's work.

- A statement that indicates that the board was instrumental in the implementation of SOX requirements and best practices at Marywood and the benefits that the SOX project has presented in terms of preparation for strategic planning.

- A statement that the board is committed to remaining in compliance with SOX and with any state/local legislation having to do with accountability and transparency.

Strategic Planning Committee   (This section introduces the members of the committee and describes the process for the planning.)

- Introduce the members of the strategic planning committee.

- Describe how the team will collect the necessary information and write the plan.

- *If applicable*—what were the deliverables for current round of strategic planning?

Environmental Scan   (An environmental scan for Marywood might include information on competing businesses in the area and the surrounding neighborhood.)

Marywood is one of five thrift shops along the Millard Street corridor. Most of the other thrift shops are affiliated with hospitals or large cultural organizations such as the local symphony. All of the thrift shops carry similar types and quality of goods, generally upscale clothing and used furnishings from the affluent neighborhood surrounding the business corridor.

SWOT Analysis   (The discussion in this section has been abbreviated for illustration purposes.)

Strengths

- Marywood is the only one of the thrift shops to also have a consignment boutique. The current consignment boutique customers are very loyal, and the people who bring the clothing and furnishings to be consigned are pleased with the boutique's 50/50 split of the selling price.
- Marywood has a longtime paid manager and volunteer staff to run the operations.
- Marywood's recent implementation of SOX requirements and best practices

Weaknesses

- The revenue generated from current operations indicates that the thrift shop results lag far behind the consignment boutique results.

Opportunities

- There are no other consignment boutiques in the surrounding neighborhood.

Threats

- Potential consignment boutique clients have expressed concern that the small space will not showcase their goods properly and reduces the potential for the goods being sold at the optimum price.

Next Level: Where does Marywood want to go? What are Marywood's Strategic Goals? What Resources are Required?

(This section of the plan describes what Marywood wants to accomplish in this round of strategic planning.)

- Move the consignment boutique to the thrift shop space and increase net revenue by 75 percent in three years.

- Reduce the size of the thrift shop operations to have it reside in the space previously occupied by the consignment boutique, phase out the operation in two years, and have the consignment boutique occupy all of the retail space.

Alignment of Resources

Current Resources and Resources that Will Be Needed to Move to the Next Level   (This section describes the resources Marywood already has in place and the resources that it will need to accomplish its strategic goals.)

Marywood already has these resources:

- Retail space
- Experienced management and staff
- Inventory of consignment goods
- Retail equipment such as showcases and clothing racks

Marywood needs these resources:

- Marketing expertise to attract new consignment clients
- Additional staff to meet with potential "estate sale" clients who might be interested in consigning the furnishings from a home
- Additional business management services and technology to manage the business operations on a larger scale

Recommendations for Priority action

(This section outlines the steps that Marywood will take to achieve its strategic goals. The discussion is abbreviated for illustration purposes.)

- Move the consignment boutique to the current thrift shop retail space in six months.
- Move the thrift shop operations to the space currently occupied by the consignment boutique in six months.
- Create a marketing campaign to:
  - Announce the changes.
  - Attract additional consignment clients.
  - Offer incentives to current consignment clients to continue consigning their goods at the boutique.
  - Reach out to "estate sale" consignment clients.
- Prepare to expand business operations with emphasis on an expanding consignment operation.
- Create a timeline and strategy to reduce the thrift shop inventory.

Summary

(Summarize the plan by reiterating its strategic goals, the resources needed, and the timeline for launching and carrying out the plan.)

Launching the Marywood Village Thrift Shop & Consignment Boutique Strategic Plan

The Marywood strategic plan describes a new retail approach in switching the spaces used for its consignment boutique and its thrift shop. The consignment boutique has garnered approximately $800 per square foot in sales as compared to the thrift shop's $100 per square foot. The strategic goals are shown in Exhibit 7.4.

As the strategic planning committee begins to move toward launching the strategic plan, it is important to focus on the strategic goals and the objectives that will support the goals. These objectives are directly connected to Marywood's resources and resources that will be needed to move to the next level. Currently, Marywood has these resources:

- Retail space
- Experienced management and staff
- Inventory of consignment goods
- Retail equipment such as showcases and clothing racks

| EXHIBIT 7.4 | MARYWOOD THRIFT SHOP & CONSIGNMENT BOUTIQUE STRATEGIC PLAN |

Strategic Goals

- Move the consignment boutique to the thrift shop space and increase net revenue by 75 percent in three years.
- Reduce the size of the thrift shop operations to have it reside in the space previously occupied by the consignment boutique, phase out the operation in two years, and have the consignment boutique occupy all of the retail space.

Objectives

- Move the consignment boutique to the current thrift shop retail space in six months.
- Move the thrift shop operations to the space currently occupied by the consignment boutique in six months.
- Create a marketing campaign to:
  - Announce the changes.
  - Attract additional consignment clients.
  - Offer incentives to current consignment clients to continue consigning their goods at the boutique.
  - Reach out to estate sale consignment clients.
- Prepare to expand business operations with emphasis on an expanding consignment operation.
- Create a timeline and strategy to reduce the thrift shop inventory.

Marywood needs to acquire these resources:

- Marketing expertise to attract new consignment clients
- Additional staff to meet with potential "estate sale" clients who might be interested in consigning the furnishings from a home
- Additional business management services and technology to manage the business operations on a larger scale

The strategic plan called for these action steps:

Within six months

- Move the consignment boutique to the current thrift shop retail space in six months.
- Move the thrift shop operations to the space currently occupied by the consignment boutique in six months.

Within four months
- Create a marketing campaign to:
  - Announce the changes.
  - Attract additional consignment clients.
  - Offer incentives to current consignment clients to continue consigning their goods at the boutique.
  - Reach out to "estate sale" consignment clients.

Within three months
- Prepare to expand business operations with emphasis on an expanding consignment operation.
- Create a timeline and strategy to reduce the thrift shop inventory.

The plan looks exciting, and Marywood's strategic planning committee is ready to go. Now what?

Step by Step: Working the Plan into Marywood's Everyday Operations

Marywood's planning strength came from its implementation of SOX requirements and best practices. Now the entire operation—thrift shop and consignment boutique alike—have solid internal controls, a document preservation system (which will come in handy for the expansion of consignment operations), and a whistle-blower protection policy. Marywood has never been in better shape and is ready to move to the next level.

Now that the strategic plan has been approved by the board, the strategic planning committee is hard at work planning for the next steps. Each of the committee members is selecting a team to help him or her complete the actions that correspond to their assignment area. Each team is drawing up a specific action plan to ensure that it has a timeline that is congruent with the overall plan. The strategic planning committee meets every other week to review and adjust the timelines to ensure that the sequence of activities will continue to forward the action.

NEXT STEPS

The time and effort that is invested in strategic planning can serve as a foundation for other vital plans, such as risk management and business continuity planning.

CHAPTER 8

Leveraging Your Nonprofit's SOX Compliance and Strategic Plan

INTRODUCTION

Your nonprofit has instituted the SOX requirements and best practices as well as written a stellar strategic plan. Now what?

You tell the world!

This chapter will focus on the ways in which your nonprofit can leverage the hard work and planning it has done to improve its relationships with professional advisers, foundations, high-wealth donors, and the community at large. By virtue of the fact that your nonprofit has implemented SOX and written a solid strategic plan, you stand out from the crowd!

LESSONS LEARNED FROM THE PRIVATE SECTOR: BUSINESSES AND SOX

Businesses have learned a great deal in their implementation of SOX. Because the business models of private-sector firms and nonprofits are more closely aligned than ever before, nonprofits can benefit from the role that SOX best practices have played in changing how businesses are managed.[1]

The trend toward holding the chief financial officer (CFO) or other senior management *criminally liable* for veracity of financials and tax returns is fully in place. Small publicly traded firms are often the targets of Securities and Exchange Commission (SEC) enforcement, and the trend is moving toward having all businesses—public, private, and nonprofit—held accountable in a similar fashion.

The risk profile of a small business or a nonprofit is being measured in terms of the quality of its SOX compliance and integration of best practices. Financial institutions such as banks, particularly those that are publicly traded entities, are expected to ensure that their clients are in compliance with SOX. Small businesses and nonprofits that have integrated SOX requirements and best practices are much better positioned to negotiate favorable interest rates and other terms. Insurance underwriters are more willing to accept a new client and negotiate competitive premium packages. Companies that have taken steps to come into compliance and implement best practices are considered to be better risks.

Best practices are becoming the gold standard for business management. Implementing best practices can save a business owner or a nonprofit executive director time and money. Before a small business can launch an initial public offering (IPO) the firm will be required to prove that it is in full compliance with every provision of SOX legislation.

Corporate boards are being held more accountable than ever before. In 2005, New York Attorney General Eliott Spitzer assessed several board members of WorldCom with a hefty fine that they were required to pay out of their personal funds.[2] Because the governmental expectations for nonprofits closely mirror governmental expectations for the private sector, it's just a matter of time before nonprofit board members are faced with similar consequences for wrongdoing.

What does this mean for today's nonprofits?

Being in compliance offers your nonprofit a competitive advantage. In the private sector, the dot-com boom and then bust was a tough lesson for venture capitalists—they are much less willing today to underwrite companies that have murky infrastructures and seat-of-the-pants management. Similarly, nonprofit funders such as foundations and governmental agencies are also looking for a higher level of transparency in nonprofit management and governance.

SOX compliance and strategic planning demonstrate a nonprofit's commitment to compliance, professionalism, and high-quality management that inspires confidence among important stakeholders, donors, funders, and the public at large. Specifically, today's nonprofits are expected to be proactive in ensuring that their board understands how to read financials, that audits, or financial reviews are conducted annually, that IRS 990 filings are accurate, complete, and filed on time, and that internal controls are in place, in practice and enforced.

Your nonprofit's implementation of SOX best practices illustrates the organization's overall commitment to compliance, but also provides specific examples of how that commitment is demonstrated at an operational level.

How and Why Should the Plan Be Communicated to Important Stakeholders?

Successful execution of a strategic plan necessitates skillful communication. The action plan should include the outline of a strategy for communicating the plan to the nonprofit's array of stakeholders. The message has to be framed in a manner that is meaningful to the specific constituency. There are significant differences in communication strategies when communicating the plan to your nonprofit's insurance professional, banker, financial adviser, or high-wealth donor.

Your nonprofit's efforts in strategic planning and SOX best practices should be used to leverage your relationship with these stakeholders:

- *Insurance professional.* SOX and strategic planning are important components of being a full partner with your insurance professional and your insurer. Insurance companies expect their private sector clients to demonstrate that they are committed to SOX best practices and to the outcomes from strategic planning. You should share your strategic plan with your insurance professional because the plan's next steps might require a change in your insurance portfolio. Your insurance professional can give you important advice to make sure your nonprofit always carries the appropriate insurance with the appropriate limits.

- *Banks and financial institutions.* Banks and other financial institutions want to feel confident in a client before they are willing to offer a loan or line of credit. Your nonprofit's SOX implementation and strategic plan are the means by which you can demonstrate to your banker that the organization is committed to solid management practices and is a good lending risk. As part of the activation of your strategic plan, the nonprofit might need to discuss the acquisition of a line of credit or a loan or other financial instrument.

- *Grant funders*. Funders such as foundations and other institutions are becoming more rigorous in their requirements. Proposals need to include a business plan, and should also include the nonprofit's strategic plan. Foundations and other funders are to nonprofits what venture capital firms are to private-sector companies. The boards of these organizations want to believe that the nonprofit will adequately manage the funding, with emphasis on results, and also want to ensure that funding is going to well-managed organizations.

- *Other nonprofits or corporations*. In today's environment, other organizations will want assurances that partnering with your nonprofit does not pose a risk for them. Your nonprofit's SOX implementation and strategic plan will demonstrate that your organization is committed to solid management practices.

- *The public*. Public trust is a very fragile quality that is intangible, but can take years to repair if damaged. One of the challenges in SOX and strategic planning is identifying the ways in which your nonprofit's good name or public image could be damaged. One of the ways in which your nonprofit's good name and reputation can be preserved is by stating that your nonprofit is committed to SOX compliance and providing proof that you have incorporated SOX requirements and best practices. Your nonprofit's web site could be a location for this information as well as information on your nonprofit's strategic plan.

- *Donors*. Major donors and high-wealth individuals want to have documented evidence that the nonprofit knows how to manage its operations and the financial assets it oversees. When calling on a corporate donor, private major donor, or prospective donor, it is important to share evidence of your nonprofit's SOX compliance and strategic plan. Your nonprofit will need to demonstrate to these individuals and organizations that it is a well-run organization and worthy of their trust and donation. Major donors and other funding sources such as foundations or public sector partners would be interested in hearing that your nonprofit is an "early adopter" of SOX best practices.

- *Potential board members.* Current and potential board members should be made aware of the steps that the nonprofit has taken to adopt SOX best practices. Include information on SOX best practices in all of your board meetings and provide the board with regular progress reports and recommendations for keeping up the momentum.

    Recruiting high-quality board members is a task that nonprofits are finding increasingly difficult. Potential board members will be interested in learning that the nonprofit has taken steps to solidify its internal controls and boost its commitment to remaining accountable to its mission, clients, donors, and the community at large.

- *Suppliers.* Suppliers and other big-ticket vendors want to be assured that the nonprofit has the capacity to enter into a contract and pay its bills. In addition to any financial statements that might be provided as proof, the existence of SOX compliance, a strategic plan, and a business continuity plan provides further evidence of good management practices.

- *Public-sector agencies.* Sharing your nonprofit's SOX compliance and strategic plan is important particularly if your nonprofit has a contract with the agency. Other nonprofits and companies who have collaborative or venture agreements with your nonprofit should also see the strategic plan and know of the SOX compliance.

- *Information technology specialist.* Your nonprofit's information technology (IT) specialist needs to review your SOX compliance and strategic and business continuity plans. The success of both of these plans hinges on the skillful use of the IT assets within your nonprofit.

- *Internal Revenue Service.* Form 990 can be completed to indicate that your nonprofit took steps to come in compliance with the two compulsory areas within SOX (whistle-blower protection and document preservation) and took steps to adopt governance and management best practices that emerged from the other components of the legislation.

- *Your nonprofit's Web site.* Your nonprofit's documents and reports, including financial reports, 990 forms (but *not* the major donor page), bylaws, conflict-of-interest policy, and code of ethics should be kept up to date for review by linking them to the organization's Web site.

Make it known through your nonprofit's marketing materials, Web site, and advertising that your nonprofit adheres to a platinum standard in its operating practices. Your nonprofit is required by law to provide a copy of their IRS Form 990 to anyone requesting this information. Posting the 990 on your Web site is a means of ensuring transparency and saving the time and materials involved in sending out the information. However, be careful not to make the mistake that one executive director did in posting an IRS 990; he neglected to remove the page that listed its top donors, including names, home addresses, telephone numbers and the amount that they donated. Once materials are posted, go back into the Web site immediately to check on what viewers would see.

SOX Saves Time and Money

Sarbanes–Oxley best practices save your nonprofit time and money and can help to protect your nonprofit's good name. SOX best practices streamline a number of common task areas:

- Finding files is easier because the filing system has been organized into a user-friendly mode to conform with the document preservation policy.

- Standard procedures are in place for bank statement reconciliation, check and credit card processing, travel claims, reimbursement claims, and petty cash disbursement.

- Employment policies and practices are documented for everyone to see. Policies on common issues such as vacation or sick leave are available for reference.

- The whistle-blower protection policy and a confidential tip line make the identification of problems less stressful.

- The posting of the latest IRS 990 on the nonprofit's Web site makes it easier for potential donors to review the nonprofit's recent year.

Incorporating the best practices reduces the potential that your nonprofit will experience a financial or other type of scandal. For example, the crisis in the United Way of the National Capital Area was responsible for a significant drop in agency donations, and also was the grounds for being dropped as the fiscal agent for the Combined Federal Campaign in the Washington, D.C., metro area.[3]

Implementing SOX best practices now will save time and money in the future. Although your nonprofit may not be affected by the California state law, remember that the two provisions of SOX apply to all nonprofits. Your nonprofit has no excuse for not having a whistle-blower policy and a document preservation policy in place.

Although adopting the best practices is still voluntary, if the Senate Finance Committee accepts the recommendations in the White Paper, your nonprofit may be required to adopt these best practices within a very short time frame.

Policies such as document preservation can be vital in helping your nonprofit to get through potential crisis scenarios such as having the IRS ask for a document, or having to produce documents in the event of litigation. Two components of SOX are already in place and required of all nonprofits. Having SOX best practices in place is helpful to ensure compliance with this new law.

SOX best practices build strong organizational bones. Having internal controls and solid organizational infrastructure is essential for growth and maintaining stature within the nonprofit sector. Organizations can better sustain the challenges of doing business if their infrastructure like strong bones in human beings is solid. Your nonprofit is putting these best practices in place while the rest of the nonprofit world is either in denial, clueless, whining, or going out of business.

SOX Best Practices and Strategic Planning Bonus Benefit: Risk Management and Business Continuity Plans

Your nonprofit's work in SOX compliance and strategic planning are essential foundation pieces for the design of risk management and business continuity plans. These plans will position your nonprofit to proactively address risk areas within its operations and to resume operations following any business interruption that may occur. A more detailed discussion of these plans and streamlined approaches can be found in the book *Nonprofit Risk Management & Contingency Planning: Done in a Day Strategies*.[4]

CONNECTING THE DOTS: STRATEGIC PLANNING, SOX BEST PRACTICES, AND RISK MANAGEMENT

Strategic planning and SOX implementation serve to establish a framework for a streamlined approach to risk management. Start by listing all of the SOX best practices and compliance activities that your nonprofit has done. Don't worry if your nonprofit hasn't yet implemented all of the SOX requirements or best practices; you can build these in later. What you already have in place is an important step in demonstrating that your nonprofit has begun to implement sound risk management strategies.

Risk Management

Risk management is the means by which nonprofits can identify, assess, and control risks that may be present within their nonprofit's infrastructure or within its operations. Much of SOX compliance and best practices focuses on the internal controls of the nonprofit as well as the systems that the nonprofit has developed to enhance transparency and accountability. SOX best practices have a "value added" component, as these identify the means by which risks associated with fiduciary obligations, legal compliance, board governance and other areas are mitigated. Risk management is also an important adjunct practice to strategic planning. Before the strategic plan is submitted for final approval and action, the plan should be reviewed to ensure that risk areas are identified and mitigating steps are included in the plan's action steps.

Risk management activities focus on the quality of systems, behaviors, and changing expectations. A hallmark of good risk management practice is learning to adjust the nonprofit's best practices and ways of doing business to be congruent with new methods and plans such as the implementation of SOX best practices or the changes that come about as part of the launch of a strategic plan.

Risk management emphasizes the quality of governance, including board membership, how the board interacts with management, avoiding conflict of interest, adhering to a code of conduct, and other best practices. Other aspects of risk management concentrate on workplace safety, adequate insurance, and policies and procedures to safeguard the privacy of clients and staff alike.

Risk management acts, as does SOX, as an important deterrent to fraud. Like SOX, risk management activities point to the need for methods to report waste, fraud, and abuse. Detection of fraud early on is essential for the economic viability and sustainability of the business—as well as the successful implementation of strategic plans.

Every Good Strategic Plan Is Also a Good Risk Management Plan
Strategic planning and risk management planning have a number of similar characteristics. Both take the nonprofit's current profile as the basis for next steps. The characteristics of these two planning processes contain corresponding emphases on communication and integration of processes.

- *Everyone is on the same page.* Everyone in the nonprofit—from the board chair to the gardener to the newest employee—understands what risk management is about and what their role is in the nonprofit's risk management plan. Similarly, everyone should understand what is contained in the strategic plan and what their role is in bringing about the strategic goals. There are rewards for compliance and consequences for failing to comply with performance expectations for risk management and strategic planning. The board and senior management are expected to model the desired behavior for risk management as well as the changes called for in achieving the strategic goals. Staff are actively engaged in risk management practices and steps to achieve strategic goals. Both are part of the nonprofit's standard operating procedures.

- *It's an ongoing process.* A risk management plan is in place and risk management planning is an ongoing process with rounds having a three- to six-month cycle. Strategic planning takes place every two to three years, but achieving strategic goals is an ongoing process. Everyone in the nonprofit has a copy of the current risk management plan and the strategic goals. Everyone knows what is expected in terms of performance, new behaviors, and new methods.

- *Partnering with the nonprofit's external advisors, such as insurance professionals, finance professionals and legal counsel.* Strategic planning as well as risk management planning includes your nonprofit's insurance, legal, and financial professionals. It is important for these professionals to understand your nonprofit and to review your risk management and strategic plans so that they can provide meaningful feedback. The nonprofit works as a full partner with these advisors. Risk management practices are fully integrated into the way things are done, the way business is done, the way the board operates and the way in which the nonprofit works to maintain its good name in the community. Similarly, the tasks and action necessary to achieve strategic goals needs to be woven into everyday operations.

Designing a Risk Management Program   A risk management program is an interactive document that is consulted regularly, modified, and reviewed at specific time intervals. The program should be stored electronically or housed in a loose-leaf binder. All board members, management, staff, and volunteers should understand about risk management and have a copy of the risk management program. Everyone should understand that they have a role in supporting the risk management plan and risk management practices, just as everyone has a role in the implementation of SOX best practices.

For example, the following risk management practices come directly from SOX requirements and best practices:

Risk Management Practices for Finance

- *Provide accurate financial documents to board and senior management.* SOX best practices highlight accountability and transparency. By ensuring that the nonprofit's financial documents are accurate and timely, the nonprofit avoids the potential risk of fraud or mismanagement.

- *Annual* **independent** *audits or financial reviews.*

    Today's nonprofits need to ensure that the financial operations are either audited or reviewed on an annual basis by an *independent* auditor or financial reviewer. The term "independent" is key in ensuring that the review is legitimate. If your nonprofit's auditor or financial reviewer also provides *any type of additional services* to your nonprofit, then he or she is *not* independent. The attribute of independence is not iterative; the reviewer either is or is not independent. Smaller non-profits working with small to medium-size accounting firms resist this mightily, but the fact remains that auditor independence is absolutely essential in today's business environment.

- *Have documented procedures for preparing bank deposits or deposits to other investment houses or other financial institutions and reconciling of statements from these institutions.* This risk management practice is exactly the same as instituting good internal controls.

- *Document disbursements and have corresponding invoices or receipts for each transaction.* SOX best practices address important internal controls as these relate to all financial activities.

- *Record electronic transactions, particularly donations via the nonprofit's web site.* This risk management practice parallels the type of internal control that SOX best practices would indicate for IT and finance.

- *Actively monitor nonprofit-owned credit cards, debit cards, and vendor accounts to ensure accuracy and appropriate use.* SOX best practices and risk management practices overlap in this recommendation.

- *Have a system in place for the confidential reporting of waste, fraud, and abuse.* This risk management practice is identical to the SOX whistle-blower protection requirement.

Risk Management Practices for Information Technology

- *Ensure that software is compatible and storage of electronic documents is secure; ensure privacy and security of sensitive material such as client credit card numbers, Social Security numbers, and the like, including firewalls and virus protection.* This risk management practice corresponds with the SOX best practice of good internal controls on technology inventory, privacy issues, and protection of sensitive documents.

- *Data storage and security—your databases and software are able to "communicate" with each other.* Data cannot be accessed or manipulated by individuals who are not authorized to access the database. This risk management practice directly correlates to the SOX requirement for document preservation.

- *Technology policy—e-mail usage and Internet access.* This risk management practice corresponds to the SOX best practice of instituting a technology policy so that electronic documents are preserved and that staff and volunteers utilize the nonprofit's technology properly.

Risk Management Practices and Operations

- *Privacy protocols to protect confidential client and donor information.* This risk management practice is also found in SOX best practices in internal controls for your nonprofit's programs and fundraising activities.

- *Protocols to ensure that programs are well managed and that clients receive the appropriate services.* This risk management practice is intended to protect the nonprofit from allegations that clients did not receive the services to which they were entitled or were treated in a discriminatory manner. SOX internal controls focuses on establishing documentation and written guidelines for programs and client services.

Risk Management Practices and Management and Governance

- Your board understands its obligations and heightened level of accountability.
- Senior management and the board understand their legal and fiduciary obligations. A conflict of interest policy and code of ethics are in place.
- Executive compensation packages are approved by the board.

Each of these risk management practices is mirrored in SOX best practices. The risk management practice of reviewing executive compensation packages is also part of California's *Nonprofit Integrity Act.*

Risk Management Activities   Implementing a risk management plan involves three primary risk management activities: risk assessment, risk management application, and risk administration and monitoring. SOX requirements and best practices have the potential for identifying problems and reducing their risk potential. Strategic planning takes the nonprofit's current profile into consideration as it identifies strategic goals. All three activities touch upon each other and should be viewed in terms of the benefits that come from their synergy.

Risk assessment is the step that determines what risks are present in the nonprofit and the potential severity these risks might bring. As you examine each of these operational areas for potential risks, *do not* attempt to make an exhaustive list. Concentrate on those risks that appear to be particularly troublesome or risk areas that have already caused accidents, injuries, or other adverse effects. Because risk management is an ongoing process, those risks that are not addressed this year (or in this round) will be addressed in subsequent rounds. As your nonprofit introduced SOX requirements and best practices, you may have identified some areas of your nonprofit's operations that had problems. These problem areas should be listed in the risk assessment report. Problem areas that were identified by the strategic planning committee should also be included as these problem areas might hamper or delay achieving strategic goals.

Develop a Risk Management Plan

- *List the risks that you have identified to this point.* Your list should contain what you would consider to be a manageable number of risk issues. For the first round of risk management planning, you might want to limit the number to three or four risk areas (see Exhibit 8.1).

- *Decide how you want to deal with each risk.* Identify how your nonprofit would deal with each of the identified risks. For any given risk, you can choose to *modify* the conditions that relate to the risk, or you might consider *transferring* the risk to some extent by purchasing insurance. There may be other ways to deal with the risk depending on the advice you receive from your insurance professional, banker, auditor, or other expert.

EXHIBIT 8.1   RISK MANAGEMENT—BASIC STEPS

Risk Management - Basic Steps

- *Take action to deal with the risks.* Once you have decided on a strategy for dealing with the risk, it is important to assign individuals or groups to carry out the action items. It is particularly important also to include a timeline for completion. The risk management plan will not work unless the strategies are put into place.

- *Prepare for the next round of risk management planning.* In the first round of risk identification, there were probably more risks identified than the three or four that were chosen for action. The second round of risk management planning should deal with these other risks. Choose which of the risks you want to deal with in this round of risk management. Remember, risk management planning should be scheduled at regular intervals, usually every three months for the first two years of planning, then every six months. Risk management practices, however, should be part of everyone's performance expectations.

- *Develop a list of risks for the second round of the risk management process.* The risks in the next round are usually risks identified initially, but not selected for the first round. These tiers of risks and the identified techniques for dealing with each risk will serve as the foundation for developing your risk management program.

Administration and Monitoring of Risk Management Decisions   This step begins as soon as decisions are made on how to treat the current list of risk areas. It is important to ensure that a "look-back" takes place to see if the risk treatment strategy is actually working. This step ensures that the actions taken in the risk management implementation stage are reviewed to determine effectiveness as well as establishing a framework for the next round of risk assessment. The strategies chosen to deal with identified risks might work as anticipated, or they might not. Unintended consequences are always a possibility. However, if a strategy doesn't work as expected, just chalk it up to experience and try something else.

Risk management is one of two important plans that benefit from SOX best practices and strategic planning. The other plan ensures that the nonprofit will resume business operations in a timely manner in the event of a disaster or business interruption. All four of these plans—SOX, risk management, strategic planning, and business continuity—rely on the others and are essential to the success of the others.

CONNECTING THE DOTS: STRATEGIC PLANNING, SOX BEST PRACTICES, AND BUSINESS CONTINUITY PLANNING

What would happen if you woke up tomorrow morning to find that your nonprofit had burned to the ground? What would you do? What would the staff, volunteers, clients. and donors do? How would you keep the nonprofit running? The business and nonprofit worlds learned two important lessons from September 11:

1. Business interruptions are a part of the life of any business or non-profit. Business interruptions should be expected to occur. A business interruption is not usually the result of terrorist activities, but any interruption can send the nonprofit's operations into crisis mode.

2. Business interruptions, even ones as catastrophic as the events of September 11, need not destroy the nonprofit if a plan is in place to manage crisis incidents and resume business operations. Many leases for new office space were signed the afternoon of September 11 by firms whose offices were in the World Trade Center towers. These businesses knew that no matter how tragic the circumstances, *they had an obligation to their staff and clients to resume operations.*

Your nonprofit has an obligation to its staff, volunteers, clients, and donors to continue operations regardless of the nature of the business interruption.

What Is Business Continuity Planning?

It is 8:00 P.M. on a Saturday night. A fire has started in the building housing the Marywood Thift Shop & Consignment Boutique. By the time the firefighters arrive, the entire shop is engulfed. Sprinklers throughout the building have been activated, and there is approximately three feet of standing water on each floor. The building has been red-tagged as the firefighters have determined that the flooring in the shop has been seriously compromised and in several places the floor has crashed into the basement below. Wiring and telecommunications infrastructure have been seriously damaged. Building inspectors believe that the building will remain red-tagged for at least six weeks.

If you were the executive director of the Marywood Thift Shop & Consignment Boutique, what would you do? How would you ensure that your board knew what happened and that your staff knew what to do on Monday morning?

Business continuity planning (BCP) is the means by which a nonprofit can deal with the crisis of an interruption in business while seamlessly working to resume operations. Business continuity planning begins by developing and documenting the policies, procedures, activities, and protocols necessary to resume essential business operations immediately following a business interruption. BCP is an important companion piece to risk management planning. A well-crafted strategic plan, implementation of SOX best practices, and a risk management plan can facilitate the design of an effective business continuity plan.

Your nonprofit's efforts in strategic planning and SOX best practices can serve as a platform for its business continuity planning. There are two primary components to a business continuity plan:

1. *Crisis incident management.* The initial crisis scenario needs to be addressed before the nonprofit can even consider the steps it needs to take to resume operation. In today's media-driven environment, a solid crisis communications strategy is essential to preserving your nonprofit's good name and providing quality information to support emergency client service.

2. *Business resumption.* Once the nonprofit has dealt with the immediate crisis, it needs to immediately begin work to resume operations. This stage of the plan needs to clearly describe the nonprofit's important functions and prioritize/sequence the functional areas that need to be in place to resume operations.

The purpose of the plan is to guide the nonprofit back to normal operations. Any plan, however, is good only if it actually works in the event of a business interruption. The plan itself needs to be in two parts: crisis management and business resumption.

The crisis management section of the plan describes the procedures to deal with the immediate emergency and then the procedures for resuming operations. For example, a procedure to deal with an immediate emergency would include the evacuation of employees, clients, and visitors. The BCP should have a section that describes the ways in which people should evacuate the building, where the emergency exits are, and where they should gather to be counted once they are outside of the building.

Other important components in crisis management include:

- *Communication* with stakeholders, such as board, employees, or clients, will be important to provide necessary information and to appeal for assistance.

- *Public relations and media contact* will be important in providing inform-ation about the emergency to the community and to provide inform-ation on how the public can help.

- *Alternative work and service delivery sites*, including employee status, availability, and notification are all-important aspects of the plan. Staff and volunteers should know in advance where they should report in the even that the nonprofit offices are not available for use.

Designing the Plan

Like any important operational planning, BPC must have visible commit-ment by the board and senior management. These individuals need to clearly endorse the need for the plan and articulate that the expectation that the plan will be completed in a specified time frame. Those individuals assigned to lead the project then need to introduce BCP concepts to employee and managers. The process will be streamlined by the creation of a cross-functional team whose members represent all of the departments in the nonprofit. The team needs to be privy to all of the SOX best practices that have been put in place at your nonprofit as well as the strategic goals that are slated for action. The point of BCP is to identify the strategies that must be in place prior to and immediately following a business interruption, whether that be a natural disaster, fire, flood, or other event.

In order to establish strategies for business resumption, it is important to determine what operational activities and functions are essential to your nonprofit. Who performs these activities and functions? Are there written protocols and procedures for these activities and functions? What would happen if the person who usually does an essential function were not available? Who would take that person's place?

Some examples of essential functions include:

- *Administration, human resources, and payroll.* These three areas address important organizational infrastructure. In the event of a natural disaster, many people find that they no longer have jobs. Your non-profit needs to establish strategies to ensure that your staff know that they will have jobs, and that they know that they also have obligations to the nonprofit such as working shifts or working in a different functional area.

- *Finance.* The function of finance includes procedures related to the nonprofit's general operating funds, insurance coverage, claims procedures, and loss documentation. Additionally, your nonprofit will need to consider how to use credit sources for business resumption. Check writing and monitoring as well as fund transfers and wiring are means by which expenses related to mitigation steps can be financed. Security procedures related to confidential transactions and other codes need to be in place.

- *Client services.* The BCP needs to include a clear description of the menu of services provided to your nonprofit's clients. In the event of an interruption, it is possible that the list of services might have to be revised to include only the priority services.

- *IT.* Information technology is essential to resuming operations following an interruption. The sooner that your nonprofit can access its e-mail, electronic files, and electronic databases, the faster you will be back in full operation.

- *Fund-raising and development.* This function is particularly important in the event of a disaster. Plans need to be in place for emergency fund-raising as well as for the resumption of ongoing operations.

What Are the Sources of Business Interruptions?

Events that create interruptions in the normal flow of operations at your nonprofit can come from any number of sources. Events related to nature, such as earthquakes, are very difficult to predict. Other natural phenomena—hurricanes, tornadoes, and even floods—may be predictable, albeit in a short time frame. Interruption of operations can also come from civil sources, such as riots, police actions, or large-scale demonstrations. Nonprofits located in urban areas can be affected if there is a severe traffic jam or street closure due to an accident, or infrastructure event such as the rupture of a sewer or gas main. (See Exhibit 8.2)

EXHIBIT 8.2   SOURCES OF BUSINESS INTERRUPTIONS

Natural
- Hurricanes
- Tornadoes
- Earthquakes
- Floods

Civil
- Street closures
- Police action
- Riots or civil disobedience

Human-made
- Crime
- Domestic or workplace violence
- Hackers
- Viruses
- Scandal or adverse publicity
- Loss of a key person

Some of the most disruptive and long-lasting interruptions come under the heading of "human-made," such as hackers or computer virus or worm infestation. Virus and worm infestation have the potential for doing irreparable damage to databases and hard drives. Sadly, workplace violence, including bomb threats, has become a more common source of interruption. The source of this violence could be a spillover of domestic violence or a disgruntled worker or client. The result of this type of interruption can be devastating for the nonprofit.

The nonprofit can experience a need to redirect its resources in the wake of a loss of a major client(s) or a contract. Many nonprofits do not necessarily recognize that this type of an event is a business interruption, but it is. The loss of a significant income stream and/or the potential to secure the renewal of a major contract can signal the need to curtail important programs and/or a loss of reputation in the community.

An interruption in operations can also be the result of the loss of essential members of employee or executive team. The interruption would become particularly acute if the individual(s) possessed knowledge, networking connections, or institutional history that was not documented or not shared with others in the nonprofit.

How SOX and Strategic Planning Facilitate BCP

Because your nonprofit has incorporated SOX best practices, the composition of the BCP is easier and faster. Part of the BCP is already in place because your nonprofit implemented SOX best practices.

Financial procedures and methods for storing and archiving financial documents are essential to resuming operations. Because your nonprofit has adopted SOX best practices, there are procedures already in place for document storage and backup. Financial procedures are in place and internal controls have been strengthened.

Backing up documents in advance will save time and promote faster business resumption. The document retention system that you established as part of your nonprofit's SOX implementation should include remote access to data files. The faster your nonprofit can access these files and the software that your organization uses, the faster you will be back in business.

An important element in BCP is the identification of resources needed for business resumption and where these resources can be obtained quickly. As your nonprofit adopts the SOX best practices, particularly as these relate to internal controls, your nonprofit can begin a list of emergency supplies and equipment so that operations can begin in another location.

Most important—keep the plan alive! Like the risk management plan, the BCP needs to be reviewed and revised to keep it viable. With any emergency preparedness plan, you need to practice, practice, practice. Stage a crisis simulation to determine how fast the staff, volunteers, and clients can exit the building, or if they know where to meet once they are outside of the building. Practice with desktop exercises so that all of the mangers will know what is expected in terms of resuming operations.

Your nonprofit benefits from having both a risk management and a business continuity plan because each has its own focus on ensuring that the nonprofit's internal controls and processes stay on track while ensuring that new risks or issues can be addressed in the routine reviews. Your nonprofit's strategic planning will also benefit from these plans as well as contribute to them. Strategic goals need not be derailed because of a business interruption. Recognizing that strategic planning incorporates elements of risk management and business continuity planning is essential in crafting a strategic plan that takes your nonprofit to the next level.

MARYWOOD'S RISK MANAGEMENT AND BUSINESS CONTINUITY PLANS

The Marywood Thrift Shop & Consignment Boutique has decided to leverage its recent work in SOX best practices and strategic planning. Through these activities, the committee has realized that the shop was at risk because they did not have systems in place for risk management planning or business continuity planning.

As they began work on executing their strategic plan, the committee also began work on crafting risk management and business continuity plans. Members understood that the value of risk management and business continuity planning lies in identifying what is necessary and sufficient. The plans need to address the really important issues and present a structured and logical method for dealing with risks that are present within the operations of the shop.

Similarly, Marywood's business continuity plan has to identify the means by which the organization would communicate essential information to various stakeholders, staff, volunteers, board members, vendors and the public. (See Exhibits 8.3 and 8.4)

EXHIBIT 8.3	TABLE OF CONTENTS MARYWOOD THRIFT SHOP & CONSIGNMENT BOUTIQUE RISK MANAGEMENT PLAN

Goals and Objectives (brief overarching goal and short-term objectives)

- The Marywood Thrift Shop & Consignment Boutique is committed to operating in support of the organizational mission by ensuring that risks are proactively addressed.
  - Marywood intends to reduce the potential for accidents, damage to goods, or other incidents that would injure people, property or the store's reputation.

   Marywood's Profile (summary of the profile presented in the strategic plan)
   Risk Assessment (identifies those risk areas associated with the listed elements of the organization)

- Board
- Staffing/Volunteers
- Operations
- Relations with the public

   Risk Treatment: Action Items for Risk Treatment (describes risk areas chosen for attention in this round of risk management planning and presents strategies for reducing the potential for incidence or damages)

(continued)

EXHIBIT 8.3   (CONTINUED)

Monitoring and Evaluation of Risk Treatment Strategies (describes how and when the strategies will be put into place; also describes the methods for ensuring that the risk areas are monitored and the effectiveness of the strategies)

Risk Management Plan (summarizes risks selected for this round of the risk management plan; includes the risk treatments selected, measures of success to be evaluated for each risk treatment, deliverables, deadlines, and name of individual responsible for the deliverables; also summarizes training needs and policies to be reviewed and evaluates previous risk management plans (if applicable) to determine the success of the risk treatments).

Timetable for the Next Round of Risk Assessment and Risk Treatment

EXHIBIT 8.4   TABLE OF CONTENTS MARYWOOD THRIFT SHOP & CONSIGNMENT BOUTIQUE BUSINESS CONTINUITY PLAN

Steps to Managing the Crisis or Emergency Scenario

Emergency Scenario Leadership

- Who is in charge if the executive director is not available; backup for crisis scenario leadership
  - Marywood has designated a five-member Disaster Response Team to lead the response to the crisis. Everyone in the organization knows that the team will assume leadership of the crisis response. The executive director will focus on crisis communication, media relations, and partnering with the board to coordinate emergency fundraising.
- Board leadership in crisis scenario
  - The board will implement specific task areas as specified in the emergency procedures protocols.
- Coordinating role of the BCP Task Force
  - The BCP Task Force will follow the lead of the Disaster Response Team.

Evacuation of Office or Other Operational Site

- Sounding an alarm: fire alarms and other mechanisms
- Evacuation procedures and primary/alternative meeting sites

  - Management, staff and volunteers and board members will recognize the alarm and evacuate the premises per the fire drill training.
  - Everyone in the building will gather at either the primary or the alternate meeting site for a headcount.

(continued)

EXHIBIT 8.4   (CONTINUED)

Communication
- Contact emergency personnel: fire, police, medical
- Communication among senior management, board, and staff and volunteers
- Protocols for the use and administration of the following communication methods are presented in the plan:
  - Phone tree
  - 800 number
  - Web site
  - Types of information given, how to obtain necessary information

Staff and Volunteers Availability Form
- Managers will utilize the staff and volunteers availability form to determine who is available to report to work.

Media Contacts
- List of most important media contacts
- Prepared statement
- Procedures for crisis communications

Emergency Fundraising (contains Marywood's plan for launching an emergency fundraising campaign)
- Strategy for leveraging media interest to communicate needs and information on how to make a donation
- Procedures for accepting and processing emergency donations (Internet, mail, in-person, over the phone)
- Procedures for acknowledging emergency donations and integrating these donors with Marywood's donor database.

Resuming Operations (summarizes the essential functions, location of critical files, contacts, and staff and volunteers assignments for each of Marywood's functional areas)
- Operational priorities: what tasks must be completed every day, week, month
- Reports or other deadline items
- Materials and software needed to complete the operational priorities
- Key personnel
- IT needs
- Public-sector contacts such as utilities, city government, and other agencies
- Private-sector contacts such as appraisers or antique dealers
- Location of essential documents and files (can be hardcopy or electronic)
- Vendors: contact information and emergency orders for supplies (can be prepared in advance based on what would be needed if the office was completely destroyed)

Working at an Alternative Location (specifies arrangements Marywood has made for an alternative location if the entire building is not available)

(continued)

EXHIBIT 8.4　　(CONTINUED)

- Mutual support agreement(s) with other nonprofit organizations or neighborhood organizations
- Basic inventory of furnishings and equipment to resume operations at an alternative location
- Commercial real estate requirements

Strategies for Financing Business Resumption (describes the resources that the organization has to access financing for the resumption of operations)

- Insurance
- Line of credit
- Other sources of credit or funding
- Estimating the cost of recovery

Timetable for Updating the Business Continuity Plan (presents a timeline for review and update of the plan)

Marywood has leveraged its SOX compliance and best practices to create a solid strategic plan, a risk management plan, and a business continuity plan. All of these plans are complete without being complex and provide the Marywood Thrift Shop & Consignment Boutique with the important framework needed to move ahead in its exciting future.

NEXT STEPS

As your nonprofit completes its SOX best practices and strategic planning, consider the ways in which this hard work can be leveraged to provide additional benefits, particularly in the areas of risk management and business continuity planning.

NOTES

1. Peggy M. Jackson, 2006. *Sarbanes-Oxley for Small Businesses: Leveraging Compliance for Maximum Advantage* (Hoboken, N.J.: John Wiley & Sons), pp. 18–19.
2. "Former WorldCom Directors to Pay $18 million in Cash." *San Francisco Chronicle,* Daily Digest, January 6, 2005.
3. Jacqueline L. Salmon, 2004. "United Way Chief Toils to Resuscitate Charity." *Washington Post,* November 1.
4. Peggy M. Jackson, 2006. *Nonprofit Risk Management & Contingency Planning: Done in a Day Strategies* (Hoboken, N.J.: John Wiley & Sons.)

CHAPTER 9

SOX and Strategic Planning for Really Small Nonprofits

INTRODUCTION

Your nonprofit has the absolute right to go out of business.

Fred Humphries is the director of social services funding for Crow Wing County, Minnesota. He has seen his share of nonprofits receive large grants only to dissipate the funds and never grow their programs beyond their current status. He has a large sign on his desk that greets visitors with, "Your nonprofit has the absolute right to go out of business." Fred knows that in today's more highly regulated environment, public expectations as well as those of funders have been raised significantly, particularly in terms of nonprofit boards and senior executives.

Fred also knows that virtually all of the small nonprofits that received large grants never worked from a strategic plan or even understood what a strategic plan was. They simply received the large grants by luck or serendipity. Consequently, they had no idea how to manage the money or how to leverage it to grow the services that their nonprofit provided. Sadly, some of the nonprofits that received large grants were simply overwhelmed by the money and imploded (see Exhibit 9.1).

EXHIBIT 9.1	TOP FIVE REASONS WHY SMALL NONPROFITS NEED SOX AND STRATEGIC PLANNING

1. You won't be small forever! Smaller nonprofits can implement SOX best practices more efficiently.
2. Utilize networking to recruit board members and professional staff. Small nonprofits need to utilize good networking techniques. Take a community leader to coffee and ask for his or her advice.
3. A good infrastructure will sustain the organization in good times and in even better times.
4. Show potential funders that your nonprofit is small but mighty!
5. SOX and strategic planning practices can be scaled down to fit your organization.

FIVE REASONS WHY REALLY SMALL NONPROFITS DESPERATELY NEED SOX AND STRATEGIC PLANNING

1. You won't be small forever. Virtually all nonprofits started out small. The ones that grew to become large and prosperous did so because they *planned*—constantly.

2. If you ever want to attract competent, hardworking staff and board members, you have to prove that your nonprofit is solid. Creative, competent, hardworking people do not have the time or inclination to deal with mediocrity.

3. If your nonprofit starts with a good organizational and governance infrastructure and good internal controls, these will grow with your nonprofit and sustain it during bad times, good times, and prosperous times. One of the reasons why the small nonprofits in Fred Humphries's county were overwhelmed when they received a large grant was that these organizations did not have a solid infrastructure and internal controls. In all likelihood, these nonprofits also didn't have a strategic plan in place so that they would know what to do if they received a large grant.

4. You need to show the current and potential funders, such as major donors, foundations, corporations, and public entities, that your nonprofit might be small but it's mighty! Before your nonprofit can become larger, it must *learn to be comfortable with the idea of being a larger and more successful nonprofit*. Having a strategic plan and SOX

requirements and best practices in place will help your currently small nonprofit to become accustomed to the types of policies and procedures that are in place at larger nonprofits.

5. Strategic planning and SOX compliance and best practices are all scalable. This chapter will show you how to scale these plans and practices down to what is necessary and sufficient for your nonprofit.

Scaling the Strategic Planning Process: Tips for Success

Your small nonprofit can put all of the SOX requirements and best practices in place as well as create a solid strategic plan. *The secret is not trying to do everything at once.* When reviewing the discussion of what is involved in implementing SOX, consider your nonprofit's structure and resources. Design internal controls based on what actually exists in your nonprofit. Design your nonprofit's strategic plan to identify where your organization needs to go next as it continues to grow and prosper. Don't expect to become large overnight. Aim for solid growth and sustainability. Do what is necessary to keep your operations running, to build credibility in the community, and to serve your clients.

Decide which SOX requirements and best practices you want to implement first and set up a timeline to chart how you will implement the rest. Being small has its advantages. Building a strong organizational infrastructure in the early days of the organization is much easier than trying to build one when the nonprofit is large and disorganized. The adaptation of SOX best practices serves to illustrate the nonprofit's commitment to maintaining public trust and serving its mission.

Your nonprofit needs to begin to make friends in the community. Your board and management need to meet with potential funders as well as community leaders. Networking is important in developing the types of relationships that a growing organization needs. This does not mean that networking is selling, pitching for donations, or anything beyond getting to know other people in your community and the nonprofit world. Take a community leader to coffee and ask for his or her advice. Invite a current or prospective donor to an event your nonprofit is hosting. Show them hospitality without asking for anything in return.

When the time is right to make a request for a donation, having a strategic plan and the SOX policies and procedures in place demonstrates to the donor that the nonprofit's board and management are committed to the organization as a going concern. Demonstrating that your nonprofit is willing to be accountable will facilitate attracting the resources that your organization needs. The providers of these resources need to be confident that your nonprofit is a good "investment" of their funds, time, or in-kind donation.

A whistle-blower protection policy is one of two SOX requirements that apply to all organizations—right now. This policy is not size sensitive. Chapter 1 discussed this policy, and Appendix 1 has a sample of the "talking points" that need to be in a whistle-blower protection policy. Once the policy is in place and approved by the board, everyone in the organization must be advised that it exists and what the procedure is for filing a report or grievance related to waste, fraud, and abuse.

A document retention program is the second SOX requirement that applies to all organizations. This policy is, again, not necessarily size sensitive. Who *doesn't* want organized files? Appendix 2 contains a sample policy plan and instructions for creating a document retention program. The key for document retention in a small nonprofit is to keep the process very simple. The plan can be enlarged as the nonprofit grows. The process should be initially streamlined to focus on financial documents, legal documents, and human resource documents. Training for staff and volunteers needs to be very simple and user friendly. People will ignore complicated processes, and you can hardly blame them for doing that. People simply have too much to do.

- Draft a *brief* policy with simple language that is easily understood that explains that under certain conditions, staff and volunteers will not be allowed to destroy documents. The policy need not be lengthy, just a statement that in the event of an investigation or crisis, there will be an announcement saying that until further notice, documents cannot be destroyed.

- Develop a list of all of the types of documents that actually exist in your nonprofit that need to be stored and archived. It is particularly important to store those documents that provide proof that something was done or negotiated, a contract was written for [X], or other documents that support actions. Legal documents, personnel files, board files, and volunteer files are important to store and archive.

- There needs to be an equally user-friendly process for retrieving documents. That means the storage protocols need to be very simple. The reason that documents need to be easily retrieved is that if a regulatory agency like the Internal Revenue Service does an audit of your nonprofit and asks for a specific document, they want it *now*.

- Do a test-run of the rules for storing and archiving the documents. Do they make sense? Are they easy to implement? Are they a hassle? Can they be simpler and easier to understand? If so, then make the rules easier to understand and to use.

- If all of this means that you have to clean up your nonprofit's files, consider this a gift. Your nonprofit will function better when it is easy to store and retrieve documents.

For many nonprofits, the cost of an audit is prohibitive. For example, if the nonprofit's budget is below $2 million, an audit may be too expensive. However, it is essential that the nonprofit's financial statements and procedures are evaluated to determine that the nonprofit is in good financial health. Your nonprofit's finance committee can become a finance/audit committee to make certain that the nonprofit's financial statements and processes are evaluated. The group functioning as an audit committee should *not* include the board chair, treasurer, or executive director. If possible, recruit one or two individuals who are not on the board—and not going to join the board—to do a short "financial evaluation" project. Here are some suggestions for a straightforward approach:

- *Ask for assistance.* Find an intern from a local university or a member of the local CPA society who could work on this short project. The members of the "financial evaluation" team can work with the intern to generate a review of the nonprofit's books and internal controls. Many graduate tax or finance programs offer internship opportunities for students who would like to become auditors. This is a potential win–win situation. Your nonprofit receives cutting-edge services (the intern is usually supervised by a professor who is a CPA) and the graduate student can list this internship on his or her resume. Your nonprofit, as the provider of a *professional opportunity* for a graduate student, can afford to be choosy. When inquiring about an intern, insist that the intern be an excellent student (with a GPA of at least 3.5) and insist on proof of the student's academic excellence whether that is in the form of a transcript or a recommendation from the student's dean. Before the student is placed, review the internship "contract" with the university. Insist that you be provided with contact information for the professor who is supervising the internship. The financial evaluation team from the finance/audit committee, the professor, and the student can tailor this internship to meet your nonprofit's needs.

- *Establish the scope of the financial review.* The members of the committee should identify the scope of the project and deliverables.

- *Use the opportunity to include some financial literacy training for board and senior management.* Your nonprofit may be small, but now is the perfect time to make sure that everyone on your board and in your senior management are financially literate. Being financially illiterate is a problem only if your nonprofit is in denial about the situation. Training in financial literacy can be obtained at very low cost or even for free. Your banker would probably be happy to assist—it's in the bank's best interests as well! Graduate students can also provide this type of training. The training can be done independently, or can be part of an internship, particularly if the graduate student is interested in a teaching career. A phone call to the placement office or internship office at your local college or university can connect you with individuals who could provide these services.

A conflict-of-interest policy is not size sensitive. Having a conflict-of-interest policy serves the dual purpose of educating the board on its legal obligation of "loyalty" and on what constitutes a "conflict of interest." Some board members are very reluctant to be forthcoming about real or potential conflicts of interest for fear that they will be dismissed from the board. That doesn't have to happen. A board member can disclose a conflict of interest and continue to be a productive and useful member of the board. Educating the board is essential, and having a plan to judiciously deal with any disclosed conflicts of interest will help to encourage more transparency.

The policy and set of procedures are easily drafted for nonprofits of any size. There is a sample conflict-of-interest policy and letter in Appendix 4.

Consider preparing a policy and set of procedures that deal with the major areas of concern. For example, it is essential that all board and senior management sign a letter disclosing any real or potential conflicts of interest. If the board member or staff member has no conflicts of interest, then it is also important to signify this on the letter. The letters need to be kept on file and archived (see document preservation section). The conflict-of-interest policy itself needs to be distributed, and each board member and senior staff member needs to initial or sign a form (which could be one form that captures all of the initials or signatures) stating that they have received a copy of the policy.

Establish a code of ethics for board and senior management. This policy is also not size sensitive. The code of ethics describes the types of behavioral expectations that relate to the roles of board member and member of senior management. One provision that is particularly significant is the prohibition against any type of loan or financial gift by the nonprofit to a board member or member of the staff at any level. Nonprofits of all sizes should have a code of ethics. It need not be lengthy or complex. A sample code of ethics appears in Appendix 5.

Institute appropriate board policies and procedures. Even if you have a tiny board, you still need to have written policies and procedures. These guidelines describe the size of the board and the various roles and duties of the board, including the distinction between governance roles and management roles within the nonprofit. The document also includes a summary of board committees' descriptions and performance objectives and the board's self-evaluation process.

Develop an organizational "resolve" to strengthen your nonprofit's infrastructure. Consider the ways in which best practices can be tailored to fit your nonprofit. Your nonprofit may be small in size currently, but can have a spirit, drive, and commitment equal to any large nonprofit.

Bring on at least one new board member this year. Your networking activities could be crucial in recruiting talented people. Target your recruitment to prospective board members who bring a needed skill set, such as finance, to the board. It is important, however, to have your legal counsel and insurance professional be independent of the board.

Utilize board meetings, board retreats, and staff meetings to present information on SOX best practices, the legislative environment, and, if applicable, any state laws on nonprofit accountability. The more the board, management and staff understand about accountability expectations, the more they will understand how important it is to invest in adopting SOX best practices.

Strategic planning should be scaled to your nonprofit's size and growth expectations. It's important to keep the planning in perspective. Organizations rarely go from small to large overnight. Growth should be managed in reasonable increments. Your small nonprofit's strategic planning should follow the template presented as closely as possible. However, it is more important to ensure that the plan makes sense, is doable, and reflects where your nonprofit really wants to go.

It is important for your nonprofit to meet with your professional advisers, such as your banker and insurance professional, to review your strategic plan and ask for their advice and input. These professionals know how you can achieve your strategic goals and can give you advice on next steps.

Review the suggestions in this book and consider how each best practice would "look" in your nonprofit. The samples in the appendices are designed to help you "walk through" the policies and documents to determine how these can fit your nonprofit's needs. Some of the best practices are not size sensitive. For example, the conflict-of-interest policy and the code of ethics are necessary in nonprofits of all sizes. Have your nonprofit's legal counsel assist you with the language. If your nonprofit doesn't currently have legal counsel, now is the time to obtain assistance. If your nonprofit requires *pro bono* assistance, contact your state or local bar association. Attorneys are expected to do a certain amount of *pro bono* work. You might also want to contact your local or regional nonprofit clearinghouse for assistance.

Next Steps

Small nonprofits are in many ways the future of the entire nonprofit sector. Grassroots organizations have been a part of American society since colonial days, and are a unique aspect of American life. In today's increasingly regulatory environment, nonprofits can also lead the way in promoting accountability and transparency.

Appendices: Checklists, Worksheets, and Sample Documents

INTRODUCTION

These appendices is intended to show you how to get started in developing the policies and procedures and documents that your nonprofit will need to implement SOX best practices. These sections have been designed in a "walk through" fashion—talking points, design pointers, and other components.

Disclaimer

Important! The language is not intended as legal advice, and the talking points are not legal recommendations. You need to consult with your legal adviser to ensure that the language and design are appropriate to the needs of your nonprofit.

"Walk Through" Documents

The "walk through" can be facilitated by the use of checklists and worksheets provided in the appendices as well as sample documents. These materials correspond to one or more chapters in the book.

As you utilize the materials in this appendix, remember that in the initial adaptation of SOX best practices, less is more and simplicity is very important. The policies and procedures need to be user friendly. The intent of the appendices is to help you design materials whose content is necessary and sufficient. Too many rules and too many procedures will block implementation. It is important to actively manage the adaptation of these best practices. Failing to have serious consequences for failure to comply will dilute effectiveness as well. Remember that the SOX best practices will serve to change your nonprofit's organizational culture. Culture doesn't change without a visible, palpable change in what behaviors are reinforced and what behaviors are extinguished.

Whistle-Blower Policy

MARYWOOD THRIFT SHOP & CONSIGNMENT BOUTIQUE

ANYWHERE, USA

WHISTLE-BLOWER PROTECTION POLICY

TALKING POINTS

The whistle-blower protection policy is being implemented at the Marywood Thrift Shop & Consignment Boutique to comply with the Public Company Accounting Reform and Investor Protection Act of 2002 (Sarbanes-Oxley). This provision in the legislation applies to all organizations, not just publicly traded ones.

At the Marywood Thrift Shop & Consignment Boutique, any staff member or volunteer who reports waste, fraud, or abuse will not be fired or otherwise retaliated against for making the report.

The report will be investigated, and even if determined not to be waste, fraud, or abuse, the individual making the report will not be retaliated against. There will be no punishment for reporting problems—including firing, demotion, suspension, harassment, failure to consider the employee for promotion, or any other kind of discrimination.

There are several ways in which you can make a report of suspected waste, fraud, or abuse. Here's how:

- Call the Anonymous Hotline.
- Send an email to marywoodreports@marywoodthcb.org.
- Submit a report in writing.

Here is what we will do to investigate the report:

[The Marywood Thrift Shop & Consignment Boutique would list the steps it would take to investigate the allegation.]

Here is how we will follow-up to report on our findings:

- Provide the person filing a report with a summary of our findings.
- Take steps to deal with the issue addressed, including making operational or personnel changes.
- If warranted, contact law enforcement to deal with any criminal activities.

Document Retention and Storage Protocols

MARYWOOD THRIFT SHOP & CONSIGNMENT BOUTIQUE

DOCUMENT RETENTION POLICY AND STORAGE PROTOCOLS

DOCUMENT RETENTION POLICY: TALKING POINTS

Key areas for explanation in a document retention policy include:

- Why does the Marywood Thrift Shop & Consignment Boutique need a document retention and storage policy? *It's required by the Public Company Accounting Reform and Investor Protection Act of 2002 (Sarbanes-Oxley).*

- What documents and records should be preserved and why? *See list of documents below.*

- Why is there a rule against document destruction? *When should you not destroy materials? If an official investigation is under way or even suspected, nonprofit management must stop any document purging in order to avoid criminal obstruction charges.*

WRITING THE POLICY: TALKING POINTS

What the document retention and storage policy is and why it is required by law. It's not just a "best practice"—it's the law, and it applies to all organizations in this country. Your nonprofit has an obligation to your donors, your clients, your board, and your staff to ensure that your organization is in compliance with this component of Sarbanes-Oxley legislation.

How does it work? In this section of the policy, provide your staff and volunteers with some clear guidelines. (Just emphasize the important issues—the guidelines should *not* be voluminous. If your guidelines are over 10 pages, consider if all of the information is necessary and sufficient.)

The guidelines should answer these questions:

- How do I start?
- What should my files look like when I'm finished?
- How long do I have to do this?
- What files should I ensure are retained and stored? (This will be discussed in the next section.)
- When should I *not* destroy files? *When an instruction is sent to everyone at the Marywood Thrift Shop & Consignment Boutique to stop document destruction. You are expected to stop destroying documents until you receive an instruction stating that document destruction can resume.*
- How do I maintain files and determine which are sent to storage? Also discuss when files can be destroyed (after X number of years, depending on the type of file, and not when a moratorium is in place).

Documents: Not all of these document categories are applicable to your nonprofit, so include only the ones that are and add those special document categories that your nonprofit needs (but might not have been on the list). Be sure to include a brief description of these documents that would be meaningful to the staff and volunteers at your nonprofit.

Here is a list of the types of documents your nonprofit would need to store/archive and be able to retrieve.

- Financial documents, reports, analyses, and forecasts
- Donor records, history, and correspondence
- Human resource records, including volunteer and board files and contracts with your nonprofit's management, staff, and volunteers (if applicable)

- Documents that reflect the sale of property, merchandise, or any tangible or intangible assets
- Documents that a regulatory agency or the law requires you to retain, such as tax returns, business license documents, professional licenses, vehicle registration forms, and correspondence regarding these documents or about your nonprofit's operations
- Documents containing information that an auditor or regulator would need to review
- Contracts with vendors for services, including insurance policies, auditor contracts (particularly to demonstrate that the auditing firm is not providing any other services to your nonprofit)
- Contracts with external clients (such as public-sector agencies) to provide services to these external clients
- Client files and correspondence
- Donor files and correspondence with donors
- Proposals in response to requests for proposals (RFPs)
- Documents related to your nonprofit's operations
- Instant messages or e-mail messages that contain negotiations for a contract or other legal agreement
- Business transactions—any document that would provide proof that your nonprofit took action in a business, contractual, or legal matter

Special Designations for Sensitive Documents

Design a *simple* classification system that allows for some of the documents to be classified as "confidential," "private," or other designation that precludes them from general access. *Again, the fewer documents that need a special classification, the better.* You don't want to have to invoke the Freedom of Information Act protocol to access your own files.

Storing and Archiving the Documents

Develop rules for managing, storing, preserving, and archiving electronic messages or other electronic data. The rules should address the important issues, including listing the types of documents that are to be retained and how these documents are to be stored. The process need not be complicated, but the rules need to be standardized—there is no room for doing your own thing. Staff and volunteers need to understand that they are obligated to adhere to the rules or face the consequences. The rules should also include steps to be taken to ensure that the documents cannot be tampered with, such as using PDF files or passwords. It is particularly important to store financial records in such a way as to ensure that they represent a true and honest picture of the nonprofit's financial profile and/or other financial description. Regulators will expect to be able to rely on the accuracy of all of your electronic records—no exceptions.

Testing the System

Develop a means by which the document retention system will be tested on a regular basis to ensure that documents are stored properly and, more important, *can be retrieved quickly.* Staff and volunteers should understand that the audits will be random and unannounced. Consequences for non-cooperation should be meted out quickly to send a message to the entire organization.

The testing should be unannounced and conducted in a random fashion. For example, one or two departments should be tested at any given time. The testing should be conducted on a routine basis until all of the departments have been tested. The results of the testing should be shared with the department head and senior management and then with the entire department. Deficiencies need to be clearly identified, and methods to remedy the deficiencies need to be presented at the same time. The results of the tests should also be made available in writing for the department's review and reference. Follow-up testing should be conducted—also unannounced—within three (3) weeks of the original test. If deficiencies still remain, unannounced testing should be done on a weekly basis. If deficiencies still remain after three (3) additional tests are conducted, then personnel action needs to be initiated.

Audit Committee

This committee should be in place no matter how small the nonprofit or its board. The purpose of the committee is to provide oversight to the annual audit, or for small nonprofits, the annual review of financials.

MARYWOOD THRIFT SHOP & CONSIGNMENT BOUTIQUE

AUDIT COMMITTEE

PROCEDURES AND PROTOCOLS

COMPOSITION OF THE COMMITTEE

The committee needs to include:

- One financial professional
- Two to four members of the board who are not also members of the finance committee

COMMITTEE FUNCTIONS AND DELIVERABLES

[The Marywood Thrift Shop & Consignment Boutique would present these functions and deliverables in a manner that meets the agency's needs.]

1. The committee is to serve as a liaison between the auditor and the board and to ensure that the auditing firm is appropriate for a nonprofit audit (skill set and experience) and to review the performance of the auditing firm.

2. The committee is to ensure that the auditor is not also providing consulting services to the nonprofit, such as bookkeeping, financial information systems, human resource outsource services, legal services, or other professional services that do not relate to the audit.

    In the past, this practice was permitted, but SOX best practices strongly recommend that the nonprofit's auditor provide only auditing services. Other consulting services should be provided by another firm. Additionally, the nonprofit should use the same auditing firm for between three and five years. If the auditing firm is large enough, then other partners or associates can rotate to provide auditing services to the nonprofit. In any event, members of the auditing firm should not be recruited to serve on the nonprofit's board or on the auditing committee.

3. The committee needs to ensure that the auditor has no financial or business connections to individual board members.

4. The audit committee should meet with the auditor to review the audit and make recommendations regarding board approval, or provide recommendations for modifications. The committee makes these recommendations to the full board, which ideally meets with the auditor to discuss the audit.

5. One of the audit committee's most important deliverables is to ensure that if the audit produces a "management letter," the issues outlined in the letter are remedied immediately.

6. The audit committee should be in operation for two months at most every year.

Conflict-of-Interest Policy and Procedures Including a Disclosure Statement

A policy and set of procedures need to be in place for the purposes of educating the board on its legal obligation of "loyalty" and on what constitutes a "conflict of interest." Procedures need to be in place to disclose real and potential conflicts of interest, and appropriately deal with these disclosed conflicts in subsequent board discussion and voting. All board and senior management need to complete a conflict-of-interest statement on an annual basis. Board minutes need to reflect a member's abstention from discussion and voting on a topic that presents a conflict of interest.

MARYWOOD THRIFT SHOP & CONSIGNMENT BOUTIQUE CONFLICT-OF-INTEREST POLICY

TALKING POINTS

Explain what conflict of interest is and why it is a serious issue. Here are some reasons why real or potential conflicts of interest need to be disclosed:

- Legal standards of loyalty require board members to put the financial interests of the nonprofit ahead of any personal gain. One way to achieve this is to identify those relationships and/or business dealings that either present a conflict of interest or have the potential for being a conflict of interest.

- By signing a letter indicating real or potential conflicts of interest, or stating that the individual has none, the nonprofit has a record of those areas that may pose a conflict of interest for individual board members. The nonprofit can then take steps to ensure that the individual board member does not take part in discussions or votes related to those areas.

- Transparency and full disclosure are very important in today's nonprofit environment.

Explain the procedures for dealing with conflict of interest:

- Conflict-of-interest letters are signed on an annual basis.

- When a board discussion addresses an area that has been identified as a conflict of interest, the individual involved is excused from the discussion and not permitted to vote. This is recorded in the minutes of the meeting.

- The board reserves the right to ask an individual who presents a very serious conflict of interest to resign from the board, or be placed in a capacity that neutralizes a conflict of interest.

Marywood Thrift Shop & Consignment Boutique
5458 Shipshape Drive
Anywhere, USA
Date
Mr. Loyal Boardmember
Street Address
City, State, Zip Code

Please complete and sign this annual conflict-of-interest statement. We appreciate your hard work on the Marywood Thrift Shop & Consignment Boutique board.

I, Loyal Boardmember, state that I have/do not have the following personal, business, or professional relationships that may present a conflict of interest:

○ I do not have any conflicts of interest.
○ I have the following relationships or business interests that may pose a conflict of interest:

List those relationships and businesses that might pose as conflict of interest.

As a member of the Marywood Thrift Shop & Consignment Boutique Board, I commit to placing the agency's interest and gain ahead of my own, and will further commit to excusing myself from any discussion or votes related to those areas in which I may have a conflict of interest.

Signed,
Loyal Boardmember
Date

Code of Ethics for Board and Senior Management

This policy describes the types of behavioral expectations that relate to the roles of board member and member of senior management and establishes a confidential means by which employees or volunteers can raise ethical concerns. One provision that is particularly significant is the prohibition against any type of loan or financial gift by the nonprofit to a board member or member of the staff at any level. *Note:* Board, staff, and volunteers should be required to read/sign the code of ethics

Ensure that each category addresses how the nonprofit commits to being in compliance with laws and regulations, being accountable to the public, and responsibly handling resources.

TALKING POINTS

Organizational values that are present or expressed in the nonprofit's mission and other supporting documents such as strategic plans:

- Mission
- Governance
- Conflicts of interest
- Legal compliance
- Responsible stewardship of resources and financial oversight
- Openness and disclosure

- Professional integrity related to all aspects of services rendered and in the process of development/fund-raising
- Other issues that relate to how your nonprofit operates

Sample Code of Ethics for a Nonprofit Board Member

MARYWOOD THRIFT SHOP & CONSIGNMENT BOUTIQUE

ANYWHERE, USA BOARD MEMBER CODE OF ETHICS

As a member of the Marywood Thrift Shop & Consignment Boutique Board, I will:

- Endeavor at all times to place the interest of the Marywood Thrift Shop & Consignment Boutique above my own.
- Be diligent in the performance of my duties, come prepared to all board meetings, and fulfill my obligations as a board member.
- Not seek or accept any personal financial gain from my membership on the board of the Marywood Thrift Shop & Consignment Boutique.
- Seek to continually improve my knowledge of the Marywood Thrift Shop & Consignment Boutique and the nonprofit sector.
- Strive to establish and maintain dignified and honorable relationships with my fellow board members, the Marywood Thrift Shop & Consignment Boutique staff, clients, and donors.
- Strive to improve the public understanding of the mission and vision of the Marywood Thrift Shop & Consignment Boutique.
- Obey all laws and regulations and avoid any conduct or activity that would cause harm to the Marywood Thrift Shop & Consignment Boutique.

Review of Internal Controls Report

MARYWOOD THRIFT SHOP & CONSIGNMENT BOUTIQUE

REVIEW OF INTERNAL CONTROLS

REPORT AND RECOMMENDATIONS

INTRODUCTION

An important element in Marywood's implementation of the SOX requirement and best practices is the Review of Internal Controls. This review of the organization's internal controls describes:

- The scope of the review and why it is being conducted. Upon completion of the SOX best practices, all of Marywood's internal controls need to be reviewed to determine if the new policies and practices are actually working. The review does not need to be overly complicated, but there does need to evidence that the new procedures are working.

- What the process for the review entails. The introduction needs to outline the process for examining the internal controls and what results the reviewers expect to see.

- The expected deliverables from the review. The reader needs to know why the internal review is being conducted, the desired results, and how the review process will be conducted.

SYSTEMS

The section on systems should describe the various systems that are in place within the organization. The value of SOX best practices centers on strengthening internal controls, particularly those associated with financial management. The report should guide the reader by describing why the emphasis is on internal systems and should express (chart out if necessary) the types of interdependencies that exist within the Marywood Thrift Shop & Consignment Boutique's internal systems. For each department, provide a brief description of each of its systems and discuss what other departments depend on each department.

For example:

- *Finance.* Describe the systems of internal controls and the systems for payroll, receivables, and payables.

- *Information management.* Describe the systems within the broad range of Marywood's technology, such as e-mail; intranet; Internet access; software interdependency; and mobile technology including cell phones, PDAs, and laptops.

- *Human resources.* Describe the required policies that are in place (or will be put in place), such as whistle-blower protection and how staff files are developed and kept up to date. Describe how performance expectations and performance reviews are coordinated. Describe other processes, such as worker compensation claims process, benefit package administration, sick leave, and vacation time administration.

- *Operations.* Describe the systems related to document retention (or identify if this system needs to be introduced), client intake and service, programmatic design and delivery, development, and other aspects of Marywood's operations.

- *Governance.* Describe the agency's governance system in terms of process for agenda development, strategic decision making, board recruitment, and staffing.

- *Other areas of the nonprofit.* Describe systems unique to the Marywood Thrift Shop & Consignment Boutique.

Recommendations and Timeline

This section presents recommendations for those systems and policies that are specified by recent legislation (SOX or equivalent state law) and those systems and policies that need to be introduced to establish greater transparency and efficiency. Establish a reasonable timeline and assign specific staff to complete the deliverables identified in this section. For each deliverable, assign a staff member who will be accountable for it. Decide what you would be able to accomplish in:

- One month
- Three months
- Six months

Set a deadline for completing all of the systems by 10 months from the start of the project. Book a "look-back" date (at the end of 10 months) to determine if further work is needed.

Selected References

AICPA. 2005. "Summary of Sarbanes-Oxley Act of 2002." American Institute of Certified Public Accountants, retrieved on April 2, 2005, from http://www.aicpa.org/info/sarbanes_oxley_summary.htm.

COSO. 1999. Fraudulent Financial Reporting: 1987—1997—An Analysis of U.S. Public Companies: Executive Summary and Introduction, retrieved on April 29, 2005 from http://www.coso.org/publications/executive_summary_fraudulent_financial_reporting.htm.

COSO. 1992. Internal Control—Integrated Framework: Executive Summary, retrieved on April 29, 2005 from http://www.coso.org/publications/executive_summary_integrated_framework.htm.

COSO. 1987. Report of the National Commission of Fraudulent Financial Reporting, retrieved on April 29, 2005, from http://www.coso.org/publications/NCFFR_Part_1.htm.

Everson, Mark W., Commissioner of the Internal Revenue Service. Testimony before the U.S. Senate Finance Committee hearings on *Charities and Charitable Giving: Proposals for Reform*, Washington, D.C., April 2005.

Everson, Mark W., Commissioner of the Internal Revenue Service, Testimony before the U.S. Senate Finance Committee hearings on *Charity Oversight and Reform: Keeping Bad Things from Happening to Good Charities*, Washington, D.C., June 2004.

Grassley, Charles. 2005. Letter to Thomas Gottschalk, Acting Chair of the Board, American University. Washington, D.C., October 27.

Grassley, Charles. 2002. Letter to Marsha Evans. Washington, D.C., August 12.

Greenberg, Daniel S. 2001. "Blood, Politics, and the American Red Cross." *The Lancet,* vol. 358, no. 9295 (November 24).

Guidestar. *How Nonproifts Have Responded to Sarbanes-Oxley: August Question of the Month Results,* retrieved from: www.Guidestar.org/news/features/question_aug05.jsp.

Hawkins, Sarah. *Nonprofits Face Regulatory Measures,* Tech Soup, retrieved from http://www.techsoup.org/print/printpage.cfm?newsid=1717&type=news.

Hopkins, Bruce. 2002. "Sarbanes–Oxley Act of 2002: What It Means for Nonprofit Organizations." *Nonprofit Counsel,* vol. XIX, no. 10 (October).

Independent Sector. 2004. *Learning from Sarbanes-Oxley: A Checklist for Nonprofits and Foundations.* Washington, D.C.: Author.

Jackson, Russell A. 2005. "There Is No Shortcut to Good Controls." *Internal Auditor,* vol. 62, no. 4 (August).

Jacoby, Mary. 2005. "Wherever Investors Go, Demands for Better Governance Follow." *Wall Street Journal,* October 17.

Jefferson Wells, A Manpower Company. 2005. *The Changing Sarbanes-Oxley Environment for Small and Medium-Sized Companies: Steps to Take Now.* August 2005.

Johnson, Carrie. 2005. "Charities Going beyond Required Controls to Regain Their Donors' Confidence." *Washington Post,* April 6.

Schwinn, Elizabeth, and Grant Williams. 2003. "IRS Outlines Audit Plans for Nonprofit Organizations." *Chronicle of Philanthropy,* vol. 16, no. 1 (October 16), p. 33.

Weidenfeld, Edward L. 2004. "Sarbanes–Oxley and Fiduciary Best Practices for Officers and Directors of Nonprofit Organizations." *Tax Management Estates, Gifts and Trusts Journal,* vol. 29, no. 2 (March 11), p. 104.

Weiner, Stanley. 2003. "Proposed Legislation: Its Impact on Not–for–Profit Board Governance." *CPA Journal,* vol.73, no. 11 (November).

Wolverton, Brad. 2003. "What Went Wrong? Board Actions at Issue at Troubled D.C. United Way." *Chronicle of Philanthropy,* vol. 15, no. 22 (September 4), p. 27.

Index